How to Find a Job

How to Find a Job

Common mistakes and how to correct them

RALPH SNIDER

First published in 2022 in Melbourne, Australia, by Ralph Snider

Copyright © Ralph Snider

The moral rights of the author have been asserted.

All rights reserved. Except as permitted under the Australian *Copyright Act 1968* (for example, a fair dealing for the purposes of study, research, criticism or review), no part of this book may be reproduced, stored in a retrieval system, communicated or transmitted in any form or by any means without prior written permission.

Typeset by BookPOD

Edited by Natasha Higgins

ISBN: 978-0-6455058-0-1 (pbk)

eISBN: 978-0-6455058-1-8 (ebook)

 A catalogue record for this book is available from the National Library of Australia

About the author

Ralph Snider is a qualified, certified, and experienced career counsellor* who assists people to search for work. He currently runs a private career counselling practice named Career Genie and is a member of the Victorian Government Workplace Incidents Consultative Committee. He is a member of Aspergers Victoria Coaching and Co-design committees.

Ralph is a professional member of the Career Development Association of Australia (CDAA), having gained a Graduate Diploma in Careers Education and Development from RMIT University. He has worked as a Disability Employment Consultant, a Careers Education Consultant at Monash University, and the Industry Liaison Officer at Education Services Australia where he updated Australia's careers website with labour market and industry information. He facilitated labour market information workshops, training careers sector professionals for the CDAA on behalf of the federal government.

The author welcomes feedback on this book via LinkedIn.

---

* Now called career development practitioner.

Contents

About the author v
Introduction 1
Job search troubleshooting 3
Resume writing 13
Automated resume scanning software 53
Referees 55
Phoning the advertiser 59
Cover letters 61
Key selection criteria 69
Job applications 77
Accessing the hidden job market 81
Job search strategy 99
LinkedIn as a job search tool 105
Using a recruitment agency 113
Phone screening interviews 119
Face-to-face and video interviews 123
Interview feedback 155
Assessment centres 157
Psychometric testing 163
Salary negotiation 165
Handling multiple job offers 169
Overqualified job seeker 171
Underqualified job seeker 173
Mature age job seekers 175
Is it easier to find work when you're working? 177
The dos and don'ts of job searching while you're employed 179

Finding work in the gig economy 181
Finding work for people with a disability 183
Applying for work in another state 189
Graduate student employment 191
Professional year programs 193
Immigrants 195
Long-term unemployment 201
Rejection 207
How to choose an occupation 209
Completing education to improve employment outcome 213
Changing occupations/industries 219
Labour market information 221
Social media 225
Personal branding 227
Job clubs 231
Government employment services providers 233
Volunteering 235
Artificial intelligence in hiring 237
Conclusion 241
Appendix A: Functional resume template 243
Appendix B: Reverse chronological resume template 244
Appendix C: Combination resume template 245
Appendix D: Work history summary for your referees 247
Appendix E: T-Bar cover letter template 248
Appendix F: T-Bar cover letter template 249
Appendix G: Marketing email template 250
Appendix H: Marketing email example for someone not changing fields ... 251
Appendix I: Marketing email example for someone changing fields 252
Appendix J: Disability disclosure chart 253
Appendix K: Percentage of recruiting employers who did not advertise by occupation 256
Appendix L: Percentage of recruiting employers who did not advertise by industry 261
Index 267

Introduction

In writing this book, my aim is to provide an easily readable, concise yet comprehensive job search information book.

How to Find a Job will help you understand what sort of work you want to do and the best ways of finding it. Common mistakes job seekers make and how to correct them are discussed.

After reading this book you will understand how to create your own job search strategy. This book will enable you to write quality resumes, cover letters, and selection criteria responses, as well as improve your interview skills, negotiate salary, and access the hidden job market.

To get the most out of this book, read it from start to finish, however reading any chapter will be helpful in your job search.

Job search troubleshooting

This chapter helps you identify where you're having difficulty in job searching and what you need to change to improve your chance of success.

Identify where to improve in your job search

The decision flowchart below assists you to identify where you need to improve in your job search – job applications or interviews.

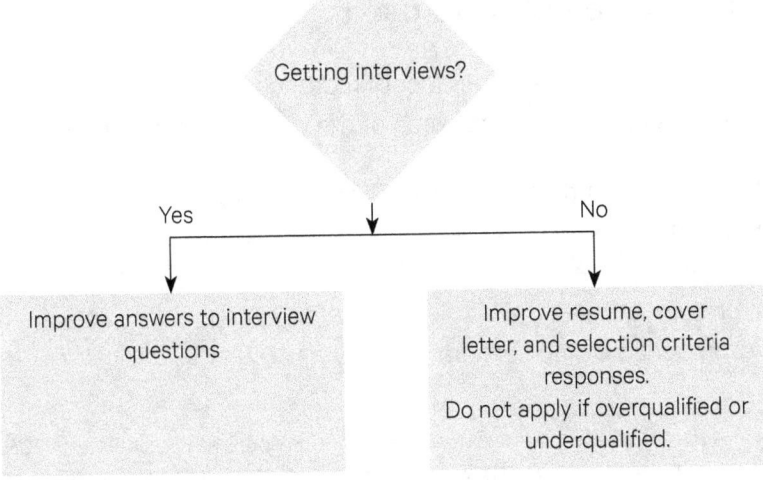

If you've applied for many jobs but have had few or no interviews, the reason for your lack of success is likely your resume, cover letter, and/or selection criteria responses. The information in the following chapters will help you improve your job applications.

Another reason for not being invited to interviews is because a job seeker is applying for jobs for which they are underqualified or overqualified. Make sure you have the qualifications/experience required by the employer. Apply for a job if you meet 80% of the requirements listed in the job ad. You don't need to meet 100% before applying. This is covered in the chapters 'Underqualified job seeker' and 'Overqualified job seeker'.

If you've been to many interviews but have not received job offers, you could benefit from working on improving your interview skills. Your job applications are doing their job by getting you to the interview. You can improve your interview skills by reading the chapters 'Phone screening interviews' and 'Face-to-face and video interviews'.

Methods employers use to recruit

Employers often use a number of methods to find candidates for their positions. Below are some of the most common methods:

Recruitment and company websites	58%
Social media	11%
Newspaper	11%
Word of mouth	32%
Approached by job seekers	10%.[1]

---

1 Australian Government, Department of Jobs and Small Business, *Australian jobs 2019*, https://cica.org.au/wp-content/uploads/Australian-Jobs-Snapshot-2019.pdf

The different methods of job searching could be grouped into two categories:

Advertised job market	Hidden (not advertised) job market
Recruitment and company websites Social media Newspapers	Word of mouth Approached by job seekers Employer approaching a job seeker Recruiter reverse marketing job seeker to employer

Many job seekers only access the advertised job market by applying for advertised jobs and ignore the hidden job market which accounts for 19% of all jobs.[2]

Whether or not you are getting interviews, all job seekers can benefit from accessing the hidden job market. This is covered in the chapter 'Accessing the hidden job market'.

---

2 Australian Government, National Skills Commission, *Survey of employers' recruitment experiences: 2019 data report*, https://lmip.gov.au/PortalFile.axd?FieldID=3193776&.pdf

Typical mistakes and how to correct them

Resume

1. Mistake: Career Summary is too general.
   Correction: Write a Career Summary that identifies the job title you want supported by your relevant qualifications, experience, and skills.

2. Mistake: Including the dates for qualifications gained a long time ago.
   Correction: Exclude the dates for qualifications gained a long time ago.

3. Mistake: Grammatical/spelling errors.
   Correction: Ask someone with good English skills to review your resume.

4. Mistake: Poorly written duty statements.
   Correction: Start each duty statement with a power verb.

5. Mistake: Applying for two or three different job types with the same resume.
   Correction: Create a resume for each job type you apply for. Tailor each resume to include your relevant background and exclude/downplay irrelevant experience/qualifications.

6. Mistake: Accomplishment statements either poorly written or left out.
   Correction: Write an accomplishment statement for each job.

7. Mistake: Including irrelevant hobbies/interests.
   Correction: Include only relevant hobbies/interests.[3]

8. Mistake: Including all your employment history.
   Correction: Include the last ten years' employment history.

9. Mistake: Including age/date of birth, a photo, and/or personal details.
   Correction: Exclude personal details except for contact details.

10. Mistake: Not including enough details of volunteer roles.
    Correction: Format volunteer roles as you would paid jobs.

    See the chapter 'Resume writing'.

---

[3] Not applicable to graduates or new entrants to employment

Cover letters

11. Mistake: Having one cover letter for all your job applications.
Correction: Tailor your cover letters by responding to every requirement in the job ad.

> See the chapter 'Cover letters'.

Key selection criteria

12. Mistake: Poorly written responses to key selection criteria.
Correction: Respond using the STAR framework (Situation – Task – Action – Result).

13. Mistake: Not responding to selection criteria.
Correction: Respond to every selection criterion.

> See the chapter 'Key selection criteria'.

Phone voicemail messages

14. Mistake: Having a funny or unusual phone voicemail message for when you cannot take a call. An employer may not have a sense of humour.
Correction: Record a professional message.

Interviews

15. Mistake: Not preparing for interview questions.
    Correction: Research the company and develop answers to possible questions.

16. Mistake: Not preparing for behavioural event interview (BEI) questions.
    Correction: Research possible BEI questions and prepare answers.

17. Mistake: Not asking for interview feedback if you are unsuccessful.
    Correction: Phone the interviewer to ask for honest feedback to improve your future interview performance.

    See the chapter 'Face-to-face and video interviews'.

Job search strategy

18. Mistake: Only applying for jobs advertised online.
    Correction: Access the hidden job market.

    See the chapter 'Accessing the hidden job market'.

19. Mistake: Having only one method of job searching.
Correction: Use several methods of job searching.

> See the chapters 'Accessing the hidden job market' and 'Job search strategy'.

20. Mistake: Not changing your job search strategy despite it not working for a long time.
Correction: Change your job search strategy.

> See the chapter 'Job search strategy'.

21. Mistake: Applying for jobs where you have no chance of success.
Correction: Apply for jobs for which you are qualified and/or experienced.

> See the chapters 'Underqualified job seeker' and 'Overqualified job seeker'.

Job search troubleshooting key points

- If you're getting interviews but not getting job offers, you need to improve your interview skills.
- If you're not getting interviews, you need to improve your job applications (resume, cover letters, key selection criteria responses).
- Don't apply for jobs you're underqualified or overqualified for.
- Some jobs are filled without being advertised. These jobs make up the hidden job market.

Resume writing

This chapter will cover in detail what to include in each section of your resume and what to exclude.

Name and contact details

Include your name and contact details at the start of your resume. You can include the name you normally use if you prefer rather than the one on your birth certificate.

Don't title the document 'Resume' because it is obvious it is a resume. Likewise, the words 'Name', 'Address', 'Phone', and 'Email' are unnecessary.

Do not put your contact details in the document header as some devices may not be able to read the header.

Foreign names

Studies show that people with foreign names are less likely to be invited to an interview than those with Anglo-sounding names. If you are concerned about this form of discrimination, you may consider anglicising your name in your resume.[4]

---

4   A Booth, 'Job hunt success is all in a name', *The Sydney Morning Herald*, 4 March 2013, https://www.smh.com.au/opinion/job-hunt-success-is-all-in-a-name-20130303-2feci.html

Unisex names

If your name is unisex, that is, a name used by a person regardless of their gender, you can add Mr or Ms before the name to identify your gender if you wish.

Listing credentials after your name

You can include relevant degrees or certifications after your name. For example: John Smith, CPA, MBA, B.Acc

Pronouns

Desired pronouns (sometimes called chosen pronouns) are the set of pronouns an individual would like others to use to accurately reflect their gender identity. For example: 'she/her/hers', 'he/him/his', or 'them/them/theirs'.

Reasons why you may want to add pronouns to your resume:

- Your interviewer will know how to address you right from the start.
- It will help you find an LGBTQIA+ friendly workplace.
- People want to refer to you by using the pronouns you've chosen.

Reasons to perhaps not include pronouns in your resume:

- You could face gender discrimination.
- You don't have to include pronouns.

If you decide to include your pronouns in your resume, the best place to add them is directly under your name. Another option is to leave your pronouns off your resume but to add them to your cover letter beneath your signature. If you decide to include your pronouns in your LinkedIn profile (see the chapter 'LinkedIn as a job search tool'), add them after your last name.[5]

Home address

You don't have to include your home address, however at an interview, an employer may ask where you live to ensure your commute time to work will not be excessive. It is probably best not to include a post office box as an address because you may be seen to be transient or unstable.[6]

Email address

Include your email address in your contact details as some employers will invite you to an interview by email rather than phone you. Ensure your email address is professional and not inappropriate. It should include your name and not be suggestive, flirtatious, generic, silly, or funny. It should not include your age or the year of your birth.[7]

LinkedIn hyperlink

When you have a well-written LinkedIn profile, you may wish to include a hyperlink to your LinkedIn profile, but this is optional. See the chapter 'LinkedIn as a job search tool'.

---

5   M Gold, 'Should I put my desired pronouns in my work correspondence?', *Empire Resume*, 11 January 2021, https://empireresume.com/should-i-put-my-desired-pronouns-in-my-work-correspondence/
6   M Palumbo, 'Can I use a PO Box for an address on my resume?', updated 14 January 2019, https://www.al.com/your-career/2012/06/can_i_use_a_po_box_for_an_addr.html
7   C Carboneau Roberts, 'Don't let your email address ruin federal job opportunities', *Job-Hunt*, https://www.job-hunt.org/federal-government-job-search/USAJOBS-email-mistakes.html

Headline

A Headline is a short phrase or sentence that is located after your contact details. It needs to be concise, exclude clichés, and include keywords. Its purpose is to grab the attention of the reader. The Headline should relate to the job you are applying for.

It is optional to include a Headline. Most resumes don't include a Headline.

Headline examples:

- Successful Manager of Dozens of Online Marketing Campaigns[8]
- Administrative Assistant With 2+ Years' Experience in Real Estate[9]
- Resourceful Project Manager With 10 Years of Experience[10]

Google 'resume headline' for more examples.

Career Summary

A Career Summary summarises your relevant qualifications, experience, and personality/character traits in a few sentences (three to five lines) and includes measurable accomplishments. Don't use a Career Objective as it tends to be what you're wanting rather than what you offer the employer. Write your Career

---

[8] 'How to write a resume headline', *The Balance Careers*, https://www.thebalancecareers.com/how-to-write-a-resume-headline-2061036

[9] T Gerencer, '30 resume title examples (a good headline for any resume)', *Zety*, updated 14 April 2021, https://zety.com/blog/resume-headline

[10] T Gerencer, '30 resume title examples (a good headline for any resume)', *Zety*

Summary after writing your resume as this will help clarify what you want to write.

Career Summary examples

- Marketing and Sales executive with eight years' experience in brand management, consumer loyalty program development, and development of associates. Strength in working with diverse groups to achieve company objectives. Most recent experience involved the development and implementation of a global campaign.[11]

- Respected leader, able to build highly motivated management teams focused on achieving revenue goals. Keep up to date with changes in the industry through continuing professional development (earned an MBA in finance/real estate and master of corporate real estate designation).[12]

- Likable and dedicated IT consultant with over five years of experience in a fast-paced fin-tech company. Eager to offer superb analytical and computer skills to help ABC Inc grow its client base. In previous roles recognized for top company-wide quality satisfaction rating (over 99%). Also, reduced client wait time by 20% and boosted client satisfaction ratings by more than 40% in a single quarter.[13]

---

11 '9+ Career Summary Examples – PDF', *Examples*, https://www.examples.com/business/career-summary-examples.html
12 K Isaacs, 'How to write a resume career summary', *Monster*, https://www.monster.com/career-advice/article/how-to-write-a-career-summary
13 M Duszyński, 'Professional resume summary examples (25+ statements)', *Zety*, 26 April 2021, https://zety.com/blog/resume-summary#it

- Charismatic bartender with over 6 years of professional experience working at high-end clubs in large metropolitan and seaside areas. Thanks to exceptional memory, rapport-building, and storytelling skills achieved a 20% boost in up-selling to all patrons. Holds a valid bartending certificate ...'[14]

- Dedicated and passionate Careers Consultant with six years' experience training people in job search skills. Excellent communicator with demonstrated expertise in developing and managing relationships with industry. Experienced in designing, developing, and facilitating careers workshops, and researching and developing careers resources.

- Meticulous and motivated student working towards a BA in Marketing at UC Berkeley (GPA [grade point average] 3.8). Eager to join ABC Media as a Junior SEO Researcher to help produce data-driven outreach marketing campaigns that will boost the company's online presence. Previous 3-month internship experience with data-driven outreach marketing. Analyzed 10,000+ URLs to identify the top 100 domains from which the company wanted to win backlinks.[15]

Career Summary examples that are too general

- A position utilising all my skills, experience, and knowledge.

---

[14] M Duszyński, 'Professional resume summary examples (25+ statements)', *Zety*

[15] M Duszyński, 'Professional resume summary examples (25+ statements)', *Zety*

- To obtain a position that will allow me to advance my potential while seeking new challenges.

If you're struggling to write a compelling Career Summary, you can google 'career summary resume <occupation>' to give you some ideas and keywords to use. Don't copy one that is not the right fit for you and your personality/background/aims.

Thinking of omitting a Career Summary section? A study found that graduate resumes with a Career Summary are more likely to result in an invitation to interview.[16]

Skills

A Skills section highlights your skills to an employer. There are two skills categories: hard and soft.

- Hard skills are technical skills learned in a classroom and at a workplace.
- Soft skills are character traits. People skills and social skills are transferable across jobs and industries.

Both hard and soft skills need to be included in your Skills section.

To complete your Skills section, start by making a master list of your hard and soft skills. Google 'hard skills resume', 'technical skills list', 'soft skills resume', and 'hard skills <occupation>' to help you. Browse relevant job ads to identify the hard and soft skills employers are looking for.

---

16   Dr J Bright, J Earl and D Winter 2014, *Brilliant graduate CV: how to get your first CV to the top of the pile*, Pearson, Harlow (UK)

The Skills section of a resume may consist of five to ten bullet points listing relevant skills. One bullet point should contain a comment about interpersonal and communication skills. Another bullet point should mention IT skills unless you are applying for a job where IT skills are not required.

Don't list a skill if you state the skill level is 'basic'. The exception is where the job ad requires a basic level of the skill.

If you are applying for a technical job, list technical skills following your Career Summary. If possible, group your technical skills under headings. For example:

- Accounting software: MYOB, Zero, QuickBooks.

You could list relevant skills for a job as follows:

- Communication skills
- IT skills
- Public speaking
- Report writing.

It is more credible if you can demonstrate where you gained or honed the skill, rather than just saying you have a skill. For example:

- Communication skills
  - Maintained a high distinction average in written assignments during studies at university.
  - Developed through customer interaction in a busy supermarket checkout job.

- IT skills
  - Proficient in 3D Studio Max, JavaScript, Maya 8.0, Adobe Photoshop, C++, Microsoft Office (Excel, Access, Word, PowerPoint, Publisher).
  - Used pivot tables to analyse and report on sales data.
- Public speaking
  - Gained public speaking skills at Toastmasters public speaking clubs.
- Report writing
  - Excellent report writing skills demonstrated by positive comments received from writing university assignments.

Employability skills

Employability skills, also known as soft skills, include:

- communication
- teamwork
- problem solving
- initiative
- planning/organising
- learning
- technology
- self-management.[17]

---

[17] The University of Sydney, Careers Centre, 'Employability skills', *The University of Sydney*, https://www.sydney.edu.au/careers/students/career-advice-and-development/employability-skills.html

Employability skills are generic at all workplaces and therefore transferable between workplaces. Being able to demonstrate these skills, where relevant, will give you an advantage over other job seekers. Delete leadership skills from your resume unless you are applying for a leadership job.

Skills can also be included in your Career Summary and in a list of job duties in the Employment History section of your resume.

Employment Summary

An Employment Summary makes it easy for an employer to see your work history. For example:

> 2018 – 2020. Regional Manager, Bank of Melbourne
>
> 2015 – 2018. Bank Branch Manager, Westpac
>
> 2010 – 2015. Bank Officer, National Australia Bank

This section is optional. Leave this section out if you:

- don't have a strong work history
- have gaps in your work history
- have done completely different jobs.

Employment History

Other acceptable titles for this section are Work History, Experience, Work Experience. List jobs in reverse chronological order, i.e. the most recent job first.

You can use the following format:

Finance Manager Jan 2012 – current
ABC Company

Key Duties:

- Used accounting software MYOB
- Wrote all monthly financial reports
- Wrote tenders.

Note that the job title Finance Manager is bolded and not the company name as this is more important for the employer. If a company is well known you can bold it.

Company description

Should you provide a short description of the company? Most job seekers don't describe the companies they worked for. If the company is not well known then it can be included, but ensure the description is tailored to the job being applied for. Company descriptions can assist a recruiter or Human Resources (HR) to understand the industries and sizes of companies you have worked for.

There are two ways to include a description:

1. A sentence or two under the company name.
2. A description which is written or worked in with the duties listed.

Don't give a reason for leaving each job. If asked at an interview why you left each job, you can have an answer ready. See the chapter 'Face-to-face and video interviews'.

Duties

You can use the term duties or responsibilities or capabilities to list what you did in a job.

Limit the number of bullet points to about five for each job. Use bullet points to list duties as they are much easier to read than paragraphs.

Try to limit each bullet point to one line. If a bullet point goes to two lines, then consider placing it as the last bullet point for that job.

Where possible, include quantitative details in your duty statements. For example, 'Wrote tender' does not say what was involved. 'Wrote 500-page tender' is better as it provides more information about the size of the duty. 'Wrote 500-page tender that won $2 million in new business' is even better.

You can gain inspiration for your duty statements in the following ways:

- Browse relevant job ads to find the requirements employers are asking for. For example, the requirement 'Have excellent interpersonal skills in all forms of communication with all stakeholders' could result in a duty statement 'Communicated effectively both verbally and in writing with all stakeholders'.
- Search your government's careers website to find a list of tasks for each occupation.
- Google 'duties <occupation>'.

Workers in customer-facing roles, e.g. hospitality workers, often list duties such as:

- operating a cash register
- taking orders
- cleaning.

but neglect to include:

- managing challenging customers
- resolving customer complaints.

Modern thinking is to view a resume as a marketing tool to position you going forward into your next job. This means that everything in your resume needs to relate as much as possible to your next position. Where possible, tailor past job duties to look like the job you are applying for.

Where a job you did is completely different to a job you are applying for, either do not include any duties (include the job title, company name, and dates) or only include the main duty.

Order the list of duties for a job by putting the most relevant duties first and second.

Choose the correct tense and use it consistently. Use past tense to describe the duties in your previous jobs. Use current tense to describe duties in your current job.

Power verbs

Start each duty statement with a power verb. For a list of power verbs, google 'power verbs for resumes'.

Consider the following duties for a job:

- Was responsible for staff of ten.
- New reporting system was developed.
- Monthly staff meeting leader.

Using power verbs, these duties could be rewritten as:

- Managed ten staff.
- Developed new reporting system.
- Led monthly staff meeting.

Starting each duty with a power verb highlights your skills and experience, improves readability, and provides a variety of words for your descriptions.[18]

Further examples:

- Provided technical and electrical analysis of transmission line faults and lightning detection techniques.
- Generated detailed test reports and worked on necessary technical documentation.
- Designed and created PowerPoint presentations for students and faculty.

---

18 '153 power words to make your resume stand out', *Indeed Career Guide*, 27 July 2021, https://www.indeed.com/career-advice/resumes-cover-letters/resume-power-words

Where possible, include what the work was for. For example:

- Wrote monthly financial report for management to see how finances were tracking against the budget and make business decisions.

This is more informative than 'Wrote monthly financial report'.

Accomplishment statements

An accomplishment statement describes something good that you did in a job.[19] It can often be expressed quantitatively. You can include one accomplishment statement for each job or more than one. Alternatively, have a section on the first page of your resume dedicated to accomplishment statements.

The framework to help you write accomplishment statements is:

Problem
|
Action
|
Result

---

19 An achievement is a goal that has been reached. A person doing something that principally benefits only them. An accomplishment is an initiative, task, project, job, etc. that has been completed. A person doing something that benefits others and the world outside them. 'Accomplishment vs. achievement', *VTHINK*, https://www.vthink.com.au/single-post/2017/09/05/accomplishment-vs-achievement

For example:

- Coordinated catering for annual staff forum, negotiated terms and pricing agreements, saving at least $30K annually.[20]

Not all accomplishment statements need to follow the PAR (Problem, Action, Result) framework. For example:

- Identified 12.5% of all bugs in Y2K testing in a team of 30 people.
- Achieved 10% more sales than key performance indicator (KPI).
- Won best employee for the month of February 2020.

The following accomplishment statement is qualitative:

- Praised for the ability to solve difficult problems independently and efficiently.[21]

How to format multiple jobs/ promotions within a company

List each job title as you would with a single job with each company, so as not to confuse any applicant tracking systems used by the company. See the chapter 'Automated resume

---

[20] '77 Resume Accomplishment Examples', *Wozber*, 1 September 2021, https://www.wozber.com/en-us/magazine/resume-accomplishment-examples

[21] University of Massachusetts Global, 'Accomplishment statement examples to help make your resume stand out', *University of Massachusetts Global*, 9 October 2019, https://www.brandman.edu/news-and-events/blog/writing-an-accomplishment-statement

scanning software'. An example of formatting multiple jobs/promotions within a company:

Programmer 2018 – current
ABC Bank

Duties:

...

Trainee Programmer 2015 – 2018
ABC Bank

Duties:

...

How to highlight your relevant employment history

If you are applying for a type of job which you haven't done for years, have two employment sections in your resume: Relevant Employment History followed by Other Employment History. The advantage is that your relevant experience will be on the first page of your resume and a recruiter or HR person will see it. Note that each section will still be in reverse chronological order. For example:

Relevant Employment History

Sales Assistant 2012 – 2015
ABC Company

Duties:

...

Other Employment History

Administration Assistant   2018 – current
DEF Company

Duties:

...

Administration Assistant   2015 – 2018
GHI Company

Duties:

...

Alignment of dates

Should dates be aligned to the left or right side of the page?

Either is acceptable.

Arguments against aligning dates to the left side of the page are that it:

- highlights the dates rather than the work you did[22]
- may leave less room for duty statements depending on formatting.

---

22 A Clark, 'Effectively incorporating dates into your resume', *Business 2 Community*, 17 October 2018, https://www.business2community.com/human-resources/effectively-incorporating-dates-into-your-resume-02129022

For example, compare the two formats:

Left-aligned dates

Jan 2017 – current **Administration Assistant**
GHI company Duties:

...

Right-aligned dates

Administration Assistant Jan 2017 – current
GHI Company

Duties:

...

How to prevent the 'job hopper look'

If you have had a few short-term jobs, avoid the 'job hopper look' by grouping similar jobs together under one heading.

Programmer (various assignments) 2010 – 2014

Or

Programmer 2010 – 2014
ABC Company
DEF Company
GHI Company

Exclude jobs that lasted less than six months as this could concern an employer unless you lack relevant experience, in which case keep the job(s) in your resume. Don't exclude jobs where applying for a job requires a security clearance.[23]

---

23 'Omitting jobs from your resume', *Resume Coach*, updated 4 May 2021, https://www.resumecoach.com/omitting-jobs-from-your-resume/

Education

Include your qualifications in reverse chronological order, i.e. the most recent one first. If your study is not yet completed, include an expected completion date. Only include a date for recently completed qualifications, say in the last five years. For example:

> Bachelor of Accounting (Monash University) 2019

If your qualification was gained in, say, 1979, then leave out the date to prevent age-based discrimination and/or an employer thinking your qualification is outdated or that you will have forgotten what you learned.

Graduates should include their GPA and/or their WAM (Weighted Average Mark) unless they have less than a credit average. List subjects in which you gained a high grade such as a high distinction.

Which qualifications to include

Many job seekers include all their qualifications, even those unrelated to the job for which they are applying. Only include relevant qualifications. If you were applying for a position as an administration assistant, it would be sensible to leave out your beef husbandry qualification as it may divert attention from your relevant skills and experience. An exception is when a job ad states a preference for a degree-holding applicant but not a specific degree. In this case, you should include your degree qualification regardless of the relevance to the job.

Include your high school qualification when you have:

- little or no experience.

Exclude your high school qualification when you have:

- post-school qualifications
- experience but no qualifications.

Training

List training you have completed. For example:

Line management training	ABC Training Company	2015
Meeting management and facilitation	XYZ Company	2014
Conflict management training	ABC Training Company	2014

Professional Memberships

Include your professional memberships if you have any. For example:

| Engineers Australia | 2012 – current |

Volunteer Roles

Include all volunteer roles in your resume, not just the roles relevant to the job you're applying for. It showcases your skills to an employer.

Format each volunteer position as you would a paid job. For example:

Secretary 2015 – current
Surrey Hills Tennis Club

Duties:

- Participate in monthly committee meetings.
- Sign cheques.
- Write monthly committee and annual general meeting minutes.
- Write agendas for monthly and annual general meetings.

It is important to list the duties so an employer can understand the role and the skills you have gained by performing the role.

Awards

List awards, if any.

Interests

Google 'interests for resumes' and 'hobbies for resumes' to help you decide what you could include. An interest such as writing a blog suggests you have good writing skills. Playing in a basketball team suggests you are a team player. Include interests if they are relevant to the job you are applying for, such as in the following examples:

- If you are applying for leadership jobs and you are the captain of the local football team.
- If you are applying for trainer or teacher jobs and you are the coach of a sports team. If you're not applying for

trainer or teacher jobs your coaching could go in the Volunteer Roles section.

If you are entering the workforce including relevant and other interests will add bulk to your resume.

Referees

Use the following format to list referees.

Referees

Name	John Smith
Title	Project Manager
Relationship	Team Leader
Phone	0499 999 999

The job title is the one your manager/team leader held at the time you were working at the company, not their current job title. Refer to the chapter 'Referees' for more detail.

How to order the sections in your resume

The usual order of a resume

- Name and contact details
- Headline (optional)
- Career Summary
- Skills
- Technical Skills (IT workers)
- Employment Summary (optional)

- Accomplishments (optional)
- Employment History (in reverse chronological order – most recent job first)
- Education
- Training (courses completed)
- Professional Memberships
- Volunteer Roles
- Awards (if any)
- Interests (if relevant)
- Referees (if you decide to include them in your resume).

How to order Education and Employment History sections

If you are a recent graduate or applying for an academic job, place the Education section immediately after your Career Summary. If you are not a recent graduate, place the Employment History section above the Education section.

When to include/exclude an Education section

If you left school early and have a significant Employment History section, you may decide to exclude the Education section. If you left school early and have no paid Employment History, include an Education section.

How to order the sections in your graduate resume

The usual order of a graduate resume

- Name and contact details
- Career Summary
- Education
- Skills
- Employment History
- Awards/Achievements
- Interests
- Referees (optional).

This format also applies to school leavers seeking work.

When writing your first resume for your first job after completing education, you may include the following, depending on the job you are applying for:

- Assignments
- Group work
- Practical work (experiments)
- Presentations
- Work experience
- Freelance work
- Volunteer roles (outside of your course)
- Community activities
- Club committee roles

- Awards
- Hobbies
- Skills
- Certifications/education qualifications
- Grades (if credit and above)
- Sport.

If you are looking for a holiday or part-time job while studying, include the following:

- Name and contact details
- Availability (days of the week you are available to work)
- Relevant training certificates
- Employment History (reverse chronological format)
- Volunteer roles
- Skills
- Education
- Referees.

Google 'part-time school student job resume' and 'teen first job resume' for sample templates. Some universities will have part-time student job resume templates on their websites.

General resume tips

CV or resume?

The term curriculum vitae or CV is used interchangeably with the term resume by most people. Curriculum vitae is a Latin term meaning 'course of life', and a CV is generally more detailed than a resume. It is used by academics, researchers, and medical specialists when applying for work because they also include research papers published, all academic qualifications, awards received, and a full work history. The format is otherwise the same.

If a recently qualified PhD graduate is applying for industry jobs, a resume is best, however a CV is best when applying for academic jobs.

What to exclude from your resume

A resume used to be a complete personal and work history, containing all jobs held, interests, marital status, age and whether you held a driver's licence, however it has now evolved. Do not include the following:

- Age/date of birth
- Marital status
- Photo (unless it's for a modelling job)
- Reasons for leaving a job
- Salary
- Religious or political affiliations (unless relevant to the job)
- Irrelevant details.

Write your resume in the third person

In Australia or the USA write your resume in the third person. For example:

> CPA qualified Accountant with ten years' experience in corporate taxation seeks new role.

However, in the UK writing your resume in the first person is acceptable. For example:

> I am a CPA qualified Accountant with ten years' experience in corporate taxation seeking a new role.

Writing in the first person can seem like you are bragging whereas writing in the third person seems like someone else is saying good things about you.

Should you get your resume professionally written?

Write your resume yourself but get someone to check it for readability and grammar. A poorly written job application with spelling and/or grammatical errors is unlikely to result in an interview.

Why not get your resume professionally written?

1. It's usually obvious the job seeker has not written it themselves.
2. Without a good cover letter and/or selection criteria responses, the resume alone may not get you to an interview.

Google 'good resumes <occupation>' for your occupation to see what they do well. Use these ideas as inspiration when writing your own resume.

Define terms used in your resume

Avoid too much industry jargon in your resume. Define acronyms readers might not know. For example:

> Attended National Association of Graduate Careers Advisory Services (NAGCAS) meetings.

Honesty

Don't be dishonest in your job application by claiming qualifications and/or experience you don't have. If you get the job by lying in the application:

- you may not be able to perform at the required level
- the company may terminate your employment if they later find out you lied.

Many people are too modest or underrate their skills. For example, they say they have good communication skills when they really have very good communication skills. Therefore, you may feel comfortable increasing an adjective up a notch, e.g. from 'very good' to 'excellent' or from 'good' to 'very good'.

Words to delete from your resume

Delete statements about reliability, punctuality, and honesty from your resume as they have been used too often. It's better to sell yourself based on your relevant experience and employability skills that are needed by an employer rather than saying you are honest and hardworking as the employer doesn't know you from a bar of soap, as the saying goes.

An exception to this is a job in which reliability is very important or where a teenager is applying for their first job. For example, a person who delivers morning newspapers to houses must be very reliable and this would be valued by an employer. So, if you're applying for a job where reliability is highly regarded, it's important to say you're very reliable and to demonstrate your reliability with an example.

Don't use the term 'coordinated' because it is too vague.

Gaps in your resume

It's normal to have gaps in your resume: periods when you haven't worked due to illness, injury, caring for someone, or difficulty finding a job. Where possible, fill the gaps by stating what you did, e.g. travel, study, or home duties. Include volunteer roles. One way to fill a gap is to start a small business, perhaps a consultancy.

If the gap was some years ago and you have been working since that time, then employers will not be concerned, so hiding the gap is unnecessary. A current gap can be explained at an interview by saying you were job seeking.

To make date ranges less noticeable don't bold your employment date ranges.

For example:

    Process Worker   Nov 2010 – Jun 2011

rather than

    Process Worker   **Nov 2010 – Jun 2011**

If you've had a lot of short-term jobs, reduce gaps by stating only the years you worked in each job instead of the years and months. Only do this if you've had a lot of short-term jobs and few long-term jobs as it can be a red flag for an employer.

For example:

Process Worker   2010 – 2011

rather than

Process Worker   Nov 2010 – Jun 2011

Resume format

Consider a functional resume format rather than the typical reverse chronological resume format if you have a history of:

- lengthy periods of unemployment
- frequently changing jobs (job hopping)
- changing occupation.

A functional resume:

- emphasises skills and experience by listing each skill and a few bullet points demonstrating how that person has the skill
- downplays work history by briefly detailing work history at the end of the resume.

See 'Appendix A: Functional resume template' and 'Appendix B: Reverse chronological resume template'.

A combination resume:

- has an expanded skills section like a functional resume
- contains a detailed work history section like a reverse chronological resume.

The advantage of using a combination resume is that it highlights skills and hides gaps in employment. Hence, it should only be used by job seekers with a significant amount of work experience. See 'Appendix C: Combination resume template'.

In practice, functional and combination resumes are rarely used. Google 'functional resume example' and 'combination resume example' if you are considering using one of these formats.

How to include maternity leave in your resume

If you have taken more than a few months off work, fill the gap by stating you were on maternity leave and provide the dates. Don't include a list of duties. If you have taken less than a few months off, you can leave a gap in your resume. You can include skills learned while on maternity leave such as time management, multitasking, and problem solving, especially if these skills are relevant to jobs you are applying for.

If you are concerned about possible discrimination, you might use 'home duties' instead of 'maternity leave'. Avoid using false job descriptions such as 'executive assistant' to avoid having to explain it later. If you did any work during maternity leave, it can be included in your resume.

Including quotes

While it is not common to include a quote in a resume, it can be a good idea if it is from a reference, a performance appraisal, or an email from a customer if it supports your job application. It is stronger when someone else compliments you than when you compliment yourself. It could be included at the end of the Career Summary, in Employment History, or at the end of your resume.

Don't include a quote from your favourite author or a quote from a famous person because it may be seen as an attempt to fill out your resume and it is difficult to demonstrate that you live or work according to the quote.

Languages

Only include spoken and written languages where the job requires specific language skills.

Job seekers who list the languages they speak on their resume risk an employer thinking that English is not their first language, resulting in the possibility of being discriminated against.

Resume length

Job seekers tend to be concerned about how many pages a resume should be. In Australia two to four pages is acceptable. In the USA, one page is usual for people with up to ten years' experience and two pages for people with a lot of experience.

Font

Use font size 10 or 12 and Times New Roman or Arial font with black text. Use the same font size and style for your resume, cover letter and, if required, selection criteria responses. Avoid italicised print as it is more difficult to read.

Layout

When formatting your resume include plenty of white space so your resume doesn't look cluttered and difficult to read. Avoid long paragraphs; brevity is better. Google 'good resume template' to ensure your resume layout and design looks professional.

Avoid using unusually formatted resumes unless you are applying for an artistic job.

Should you send your job application documents in Word or PDF format?

Advantages of Word format:

- Recruiters can amend your resume to remove personal contact details before forwarding it to the employer, so the employer cannot contact you.
- Older applicant tracking systems used by HR and recruiters to automate and speed up the identification of suitable job seekers can read details off a Word document (but not a PDF).

Advantages of PDF format:

- Your resume format will remain the same regardless of the device used to read your resume.

Filename

Name your resume filename with your name, e.g. 'John Smith resume', so employers/recruiters don't have to rename your resume file. Do the same for cover letters and selection criteria responses.

How many resumes do you need?

Many job seekers make the mistake of having one resume which they use to apply for different types of jobs. For example, consider a job seeker with experience as an administration assistant who recently qualified as a counsellor. Combining their administration experience with their counselling qualification in the one resume results in a resume that tries to do two things rather than one. It may result in a confusing Career Summary. An employer might wonder why a person applying for an administration assistant job has recently qualified as a counsellor.

If a job seeker wants to apply for two different types of jobs, e.g. administrative assistant and counsellor, the best approach is to write two resumes: one highlighting relevant administration assistant skills and experience while deleting the counselling qualification, and a second resume highlighting the counselling qualification and downplaying the administration assistant experience.

How do you downplay administration assistant experience? By including duties for the administration assistant jobs which highlight communication, discussion, facilitation, and decision-making parts of the job that are relevant to counselling work and excluding or minimising the administrative duties. Perhaps the last duty for the job could briefly mention administrative duties.

To summarise, for each type of job you apply for you need a tailored resume.

How to rewrite your resume if you are changing occupation

Use a combination resume format. See 'Appendix C: Combination resume template'.

The key is to identify your transferable skills in your current occupation that will be needed in your new occupation.

Key sections of the resume can be changed in the following ways.

- **Career Summary**

Write the Career Summary after you've written the rest of the resume. Include relevant accomplishments and/or relevant transferable skills. Don't state your current job title or occupation in your Career Summary.

As an example of a career change Career Summary, consider a taxi driver applying for a call centre operator job:

> Call Centre Operator with excellent skills in managing difficult customers, resolving customer complaints, and performing financial transactions seeks challenging new role.

- **Skills**

Read the job ad and list the skills required. Think of examples from your work history which you can use to demonstrate you have those skills.

- **Employment History**

Where possible, tailor past job duties to look like the duties of the job you are applying for. For our example of a taxi driver applying for a call centre operator job, you might think that there are no transferable skills between these two occupations.

Job duties for a taxi driver are:

- safe driving record
- excellent knowledge of city and suburban streets
- good mechanical ability.

However, for a taxi driver wanting to highlight their transferable skills into a call centre operator job, the duties for a taxi driver could be changed to:

- manages challenging customers
- resolves customer complaints
- performs electronic financial transactions.

Note that each of these duties is performed by call centre operators.

As much as possible, everything in your resume needs to be tailored to the job you're applying for.

- **Education**

Refer to the chapter 'Completing education to improve employment outcome'.

- **Interests**

Only include interests if relevant to the job you're applying for.

How to rewrite your resume if you don't have relevant transferable skills

For example, a professional needing to find work quickly may turn to factory work. Transferable skills will include employability skills (see the 'Skills' section in the chapter 'Resume writing') but not technical skills. There won't be enough transferable skills between the professional role and a factory worker.

Browse a careers website to find the skills, abilities, and activities needed for a factory worker. Include skills such as being able to operate machinery, physical fitness, reading and writing, aptitude for monitoring quality, problem solving, and operational monitoring.

Resume writing key points

- A resume is a marketing tool to get you a job, not a complete work history, hence a resume must be tailored for each type of job you apply for.
- A Career Summary states your relevant qualifications, experience, and personality/character traits.
- When you list a skill, demonstrate you have the skill by stating how you obtained it.
- Start job duty statements with a power verb.
- Include an accomplishment statement for each job, ideally expressed quantitatively. Alternatively, have a section on the first page of your resume listing all your accomplishment statements.
- Include details of volunteer roles as you would for a paid job.
- Where possible fill gaps in your resume by stating what you did.
- Exclude jobs that lasted less than six months unless you lack relevant experience or job requires a security clearance.
- Consider a functional resume format if you have lengthy periods of unemployment or frequently change jobs.
- Consider a combination resume format to highlight skills and hide employment gaps or when changing occupation.

Automated resume scanning software

Applicant tracking systems (ATS) are automated resume scanning software used by HR and recruiters to enable faster identification of suitable job seekers by breaking resumes or job seekers' answers to questions into categories that are stored in a searchable database.

What not to include in your resume

Graphs, pie charts, and illustrations are not readable by ATS so don't include them in your resume.

Trying to beat the ATS

Amending your resume to include skills/keywords for each job application to be selected by the ATS is too much work. If your job application is not a strong response to the job ad, it's unlikely to be successful even if you try to fool the ATS by including skills/keywords. If your application is strong, you don't need to amend your resume using keywords from the job ad.

Trying to beat the ATS by using white font

In an attempt to include keywords, some job seekers add the job ad to the resume using white font in an attempt to beat the ATS. However, ATS are now better at reading resumes, and if the recruiter changes all text to black font then your relationship with that recruiter is likely to end.

Referees

Referees do not have to be listed in your resume. You can state in your resume that referees will be 'provided at interview' or you can exclude the referee section. If you choose not to list referees in your resume, then email them to the employer upon request after an interview. If the job ad requests you supply referees as part of the job application, include them.

Provide two or three referees. Some employers ask for two referees and others ask for three. Don't provide three if the employer asks for two. Use your strongest two of the three.

If your referees are overseas, give the employer their email addresses and the best hours to contact them in the employer's time zone.

Ask each of your potential referees for permission to be your referee before attending any interviews. This will ensure that when they are contacted by an employer, they will be prepared to speak strongly on your behalf.

Referees should include at least one former team leader/manager. Next best is a colleague you worked with. Your referees do not have to be from your most recent job. If you are currently working while you search for work, don't use anyone from your current company as a referee. You don't want your current team leader finding out that you are looking for another job. If none of your referees are former team leaders or managers, this might be a red flag for a prospective employer.

If a referee is not prepared to be a strong supporter of you, do not include them. If you are not sure if they will be a strong supporter, or to help them prepare to speak about you, give them a one-page summary of your work history when you were working for them. See 'Appendix D: Work history summary for your referees'. Check your referees agree with the summary you have prepared for them.

If an interview goes well, you can phone your referees to let them know that they might receive a call from an employer.

Legally, an employer can only perform referee checks on referees provided by the job seeker.

After you get a job, thank your referees.

What to do if you don't have any referees

One option is to do some voluntary work and ask the volunteer team leader to be your referee. Another option is to ask someone who knows you personally to be a referee but not a friend or family member unless you have done work for them. A recent graduate can ask a lecturer, professor, or tutor. A community leader is another option. An employer before a career break is acceptable.

Sometimes, even if you haven't performed well in a job, your team leader will still be willing to be your referee. If your team leader from your last job will not be your referee, then hopefully a colleague from that company or a team leader from a previous job will.

What should you do if you don't have your team leader from your last job as a referee, either because they refused or you did not want to ask them? If asked by an employer or recruiter why you have not included your most recent team leader as a referee, say that the referees you have chosen will speak strongly on your behalf.

Some companies you worked for may no longer operate or refuse to give references. One option is to use a work colleague who can speak strongly on your behalf.

In place of referees, some employers might accept a written reference, a recent performance review or an award, or be prepared to negotiate a longer probationary period. Sometimes employers don't ask for referees and don't perform referee checks, especially small companies without HR personnel.

Written references

Australian employers prefer to contact referees by phone. If you have a written reference from a past employer, including a copy of the reference in your job application cannot do any harm.

Referees key points

- Ensure you have two or three referees.
- Ask permission from people to be your referees.
- Ensure at least one referee is a former team leader or manager.
- If you don't have any referees, do volunteer roles to obtain a referee where you volunteer or ask a personal contact who is not a friend or family member.
- Referees do not have to be from your last workplace; they can be from earlier workplaces.

Phoning the advertiser

Often job ads include a contact name and phone number so you can ask questions to find out more about the job. It's a good idea to phone to find out more about the duties of the position, especially if you have some questions arising out of reading the job ad or the position description. It shows you are interested in the job.

You can ask the contact person the key priorities of the job in the first six months and use this information in the interview, by stating how you would approach the role and asking if they are happy with your approach. During the phone conversation, the contact person may emphasise some aspects of the job which might then direct your interview preparation.

The contact person will probably ask you about your background so you need to be prepared with an answer. It can be like the interview question 'Tell us about yourself'. See the chapter 'Face-to-face and video interviews'.

You can ask if the job is new or vacated. If the job has been advertised several times, you could ask for the reason. You might decide not to apply or attend an interview if there is a high staff turnover.

If you find out from the contact person that the person currently in the job has been seconded from another role, you may decide not to put in as much time applying or decide not to apply because the person seconded into the role is likely to apply for the job and would have an advantage. However, if the job really interests you, apply anyway.

Sometimes an organisation will already know who they want to fill a vacancy but they still advertise and hold interviews to satisfy their governance requirements to advertise all jobs.

Phoning an employer to show interest in the job only for the purpose of gaining an advantage over other applicants is unlikely to succeed because the job application will likely determine who is invited to the interview.

If the employer does not include their contact details in the ad, do not contact them as this indicates that they don't want to be contacted.

Phoning the advertiser key points

- Phone the advertiser if you have any questions about the job. What you learn about the job may assist you with your interview preparation and in the interview.
- If the advertiser has not included their contact details in the job ad, do not contact them.

Cover letters

This chapter explains how to tailor cover letters to the job you're applying for.

Many job seekers make the mistake of using one cover letter for all their job applications. Cover letters need to be tailored to the job you are applying for by including qualifications and experience that match the employer's requirements.

Letter structure

A cover letter contains the following sections and should be one page in length:

- Contact information (name, address, phone number, email address).
- Introduction (stating the job you are applying for).
- Why you want to work for the company.
    - My skill set is very relevant to the job because …
    - I would appreciate the opportunity to work for a company that …
    - This job fits with my career plan which is to …
- Relevant qualifications, skills, and experience.

- Concluding paragraph (suggesting an interview as the next step).

Salutation

Address the cover letter to a person if you know the name of the employer, otherwise use 'Dear Hiring Manager'.

First paragraph

Start your cover letter by stating the job you're applying for. For example:

I am excited to apply for the Employment Consultant job, reference 0124, advertised on SEEK. I attach my resume in support of my application. The description of the job meets my current career goal to work within a careers environment specifically helping people with disabilities.

Middle paragraphs

These paragraphs describe why you want to work for the company. Include your qualifications, skills, and experience that relate to the requirements listed in the job ad. Too many job seekers include experience that is not relevant to the job in their cover letter.

Concluding paragraph

Finish your cover letter with the suggestion that there is more the employer can learn about you during an interview and provide your best contact. For example:

I would welcome the opportunity to meet with you personally at an interview to provide you with further details of my qualifications and professional skills in relation to this application. I can be contacted on … … …

Yours sincerely,

<your name>

Including quotes

While rare, it is good to include a quote in your cover letter from a reference, a performance appraisal, or an email from a customer if it supports your application. It is stronger when someone else compliments you than when you compliment yourself.

As aforementioned in the 'Resume writing' chapter, don't include a quote from your favourite author or a quote from a famous person because it may be seen as an attempt to fill out your cover letter and it is difficult to demonstrate that you live or work according to the quote.

An alternative to the cover letter is the T-Bar cover letter format.

T-Bar cover letter

The author recommends using the T-Bar cover letter format which lists each job requirement and your matching skills and experience. See example T-Bar cover letter templates in Appendix E and Appendix F. Unlike a standard cover letter, it's okay for a T-Bar cover letter to be more than one page long.

Let's use the following two job ads as examples. The first job ad has bullet-pointed statements which list the employer's requirements. The second ad embeds the requirements in the ad's paragraphs.

Example 1:

Office Administration Assistant Part-Time

REPLACEMENT POSITION

3 days per week – Monday to Wednesday

Bentleigh College is an independent secondary school for girls.

We are passionate about young women and their success. We empower the learner, inspire a global consciousness and are at the forefront of innovative learning. We Believe! We Achieve!

To continue growing our impressive achievements, we now seek to appoint an excellent administration assistant. The successful interviewee will be the first point of contact for student, staff and parent enquiries. With a spirit of openness of heart and a flexibility to serve our young women, staff and parents, the person in this role will live the values of the school.

This position is a part-time position 0.6 FTE and is scheduled to commence Monday 11 May 2020.

The successful interviewee will:

- have an understanding of and commitment to education
- provide outstanding administrative service to students, parents and teachers

- have excellent interpersonal skills in all forms of communication with all stakeholders
- provide high-level administrative support, particularly for the smooth operations of student data in all forms
- be confident with IT software and be willing to learn the school's data systems
- have excellent secretarial skills, including a sound knowledge of Microsoft packages
- support the general administration and clerical work within the school
- be comfortable working with student medical needs.

A current Working with Children Check (WWCC) is required and a current First Aid qualification would be an advantage.

A role description and selection criteria are available on the College website as of 4.00pm Tuesday 21 April 2020 at www.bentleighcollege.vic.edu.au Applications including a cover letter, resume and the contact details of three referees to be emailed to:

The Principal at principal@bentleighcollege.vic.edu.au.

Applications close on Wednesday 29 April 2020.[23]

How to respond to the job ad

Include the bullet-pointed requirements in the T-Bar cover letter and your responses so that the employer can clearly see your response to each of their requirements.

---

23 seek.com.au (amended)

Additionally, you need to state if you have a current WWCC and a current first aid qualification.

Example 2:

Administrative Assistant

- Located at our Malvern Campus
- Full-time, fixed term role
- Support our team of Associate Directors

Bayside Grammar School is one of the world's leading coeducational boarding and day schools, offering exceptional education to all of its students, from Early Learning to Year 12.

We seek to appoint an Administrative Assistant with excellent communication, interpersonal and organisational skills to this full-time, fixed term role (two-year contract). This role, located at our Malvern campus, will support the fundraising activities of our team of Associate Directors within the Community Relations Department.

Applicants should be proficient in the use of the Microsoft Office suite (Word, Outlook, PowerPoint and Excel), and Database systems.

Remuneration will be in accordance with the Bayside Grammar School Salary Scale.

For further details and/or to apply online, visit the employment opportunities page on our website: www.bgs.vic.edu.au/careers

Applications close at 4.00pm on Tuesday 28 April 2015.[24]

How to respond to the job ad

In this second example, you need to identify the employer's requirements. The requirements are:

- excellent communication, interpersonal and organisational skills
- support the fundraising activities of our team of Associate Directors within the Community Relations Department
- be proficient in the use of the Microsoft Office suite (Word, Outlook, PowerPoint and Excel), and Database systems.

In response to the requirement 'excellent communication, interpersonal and organisational skills', it is not enough to state, 'I have excellent communication, interpersonal and organisational skills'. You need to be able to demonstrate how you have these skills. You might say, 'I have excellent communication skills from working in a call centre. My interpersonal skills were honed when I worked in a team at a fast-food shop. I developed organisational skills working in a busy job where I provided administrative support to three managers.'

Where you don't have experience in a job requirement, for example, experience with the accounting software Zero, you could state that you have experience with MYOB, a similar accounting package, and that you are a fast learner. Where you

---

24 seek.com.au (amended)

have no experience in a job requirement, you might want to leave it off your cover letter or state you are a fast learner and state your relevant transferrable skills.

Concluding paragraph

Finish your T-Bar cover letter in the same way as a regular cover letter. For example:

> I would welcome the opportunity to meet with you personally at an interview to provide you with further details of my qualifications and professional skills in relation to this application. I can be contacted on ... ...
>
> Yours sincerely,
>
> <your name>

Cover letters key points

- Cover letters need to be tailored to the requirements in the job ad.
- A T-Bar cover letter format lists each requirement stated in the job ad and the job seeker responds to each requirement by stating their relevant qualifications, skills and experiences.

Key selection criteria

This chapter explains what key selection criteria are, their importance, and how to respond to them.

What are key selection criteria?

Key selection criteria (KSC), also known as selection criteria, are statements in the job ad or position description[25] listing the skills and experience required by an employer. The words 'Selection Criteria' will precede the statements, so you can easily identify them.

For example:

- Demonstrated skills in working with and knowledge of Microsoft Office programs including Word, Excel, and Outlook.
- Strong organisational and problem-solving skills.

---

25 A Position Description is a written account of all the duties and responsibilities involved in a particular job or position. https://www.collinsdictionary.com/dictionary/english/job-description (amended)

How to respond to key selection criteria

A job seeker needs to respond to each selection criterion listed in the key selection criteria. Typically, an employer will list six to twelve criteria.

The length of a response to each criterion should be between one-half and three-quarters of a page. Some employers limit the number of words a job seeker can use to respond to a criterion. Check the job application instructions to see if there is a word limit.

Respond to selection criteria by using the STAR framework. STAR is an acronym that stands for:

- S – Situation
- T – Task
- A – Action
- R – Result.

Situation

- Description of the job where you used the skills or gained the experience.

Task

- What did the task involve?

Action

- What you did and how you did it. (Not what *we* did.)

Result

- What did you achieve? What was the result? Quantify if possible.

A response to a selection criterion can include an opening statement of claim as to how you fulfil the criterion, followed by the STAR framework response.

Example selection criterion and response

Selection criterion

Problem solving – Seeks all relevant facts. Liaises with stakeholders. Analyses issues from different perspectives and draws sound inferences from available data. Identifies and proposes workable solutions.

Response

Problem solving has been a critical part of my roles over the past five years. While working as Customer Complaints Officer at Acme Department Stores, I dealt with a variety of problems. While many could be resolved easily, two to three per week were more complex and required a detailed process to resolve. I had to investigate what had happened from the staff and customer's points of view, clarify the facts, and work out what had gone wrong and why. I then had to propose suitable solutions and negotiate a mutually satisfactory outcome. I was often commended by my manager for my sensitive handling and speedy resolution of these problems. Less than one per cent of complaints had to be escalated.[26]

---

26 'How to write key selection criteria', *Victoria / Careers.VIC*, https://careers.vic.gov.au/how-to-reply-to-selection-criteria

Analysing the above response using the STAR framework

The statement of claim is:

Problem solving has been a critical part of my roles over the past five years.

- **Situation:** While working as Customer Complaints Officer at Acme Department Stores.
- **Task:** I dealt with a variety of problems. While many could be resolved easily, two to three per week were more complex and required a detailed process to resolve.
- **Action:** I had to investigate what had happened from the staff and customer's points of view, clarify the facts, and work out what had gone wrong and why. I then had to propose suitable solutions and negotiate a mutually satisfactory outcome.
- **Result:** I was often commended by my manager for my sensitive handling and speedy resolution of these problems. Less than one per cent of complaints had to be escalated.

STAR response tips

When responding, make it clear what **you** did. Don't use the word 'we'.

Use relevant recent examples where possible. While workplace examples are preferred, you can use examples from volunteer roles. Graduates can use examples from work experience, extra-curricular activities, or university experience.

Common terms used: knowledge, understanding, experience

Many selection criteria include one of the following terms: knowledge, understanding, or experience. If an employer is asking for knowledge about a certain topic, e.g. National Standards for Disability Services, they don't require you to have experience. If you don't have the knowledge they are asking for, research it online to provide an answer. Similarly, understanding requires no experience.

Desirable selection criteria

Sometimes selection criteria are listed under two headings: essential and desirable. Respond to all selection criteria, including those listed as desirable.

How to respond if you don't meet a selection criterion

1. State you have similar transferable experience and give the details.
2. State you are a quick learner.
3. Carry out the necessary research to get the knowledge and/or understanding required.

Responding to multiple criteria within a selection criterion

If there are multiple criteria in the one selection criterion, you'll need to address each separately.

For example, for the selection criterion, 'Excellent verbal and written communication skills' you will need to demonstrate both your verbal and your written communication skills with an example of each.

The importance of responding to key selection criteria

Even if a job seeker has the best resume and cover letter, they will not get to an interview if they write a poor selection criteria response or if they do not respond to the selection criteria. To reduce your job application workload, if a job application requires both a selection criteria response and a cover letter, then you might save time by writing a one-page cover letter rather than a T-Bar cover letter, as the selection criteria response is more likely to determine who gets invited to an interview.

Responses to selection criteria are very difficult to write well. It is essential that the responses are well written and contain good grammar. If writing and grammar are not your strengths, ask someone who is good at writing to proofread what you have written.

Respond to key selection criteria in a separate document to your resume and cover letter. Include your name, the job title, and the reference number of the job you're applying for. Then state each criterion in bold print followed by your response.

Key selection criteria key points

- Some job ads require you to respond to key selection criteria.
- Respond to selection criteria by using the STAR framework (Situation – Task – Action – Result).
- Respond to both essential and desirable criteria.
- Where a selection criterion has multiple components, respond to each part.

Job applications

This chapter includes tips for completing job application forms, and seeking feedback on unsuccessful job applications.

When to apply for jobs

When applying for jobs, don't wait until close to the closing date before applying as some companies desperate to fill a position may start interviewing prior to the closing date.

If you do miss the closing date, apply anyway. Apply direct to the company if applying via their website is no longer possible, because the hiring manager may accept late applications.

Job application forms

Before starting to complete the job application form, read the application form, the job ad, the position description, and any instructions. Identify which questions you need to answer and which are optional. Complete each answer in a separate document before copying your answer to the application form. Keep within any word limit. Check what you have written for grammatical and spelling errors.

How to handle salary in a job application form

- Leave it blank if you can.
- Type 'Negotiable' if the field will accept non-numerical responses.
- Type '0' if the field only accepts numerical responses and in another section type 'Salary is negotiable'.

Where to apply

If you are asked to fill out an application form on a job board, check if the job is also advertised on the company's website. It may be possible to apply through the company's website without filling out a form. If both websites require filling out a form, apply via the company's website because the quality of the applications is likely to be higher via the company's website than via the job board.[27]

Should you apply via LinkedIn or a company website? See the chapter 'LinkedIn as a job search tool'.

Check your job application for consistency

Ensure consistency across your job application documents (resume, cover letter, and selection criteria response) and LinkedIn profile regarding the number of years you worked in an occupation or industry and other details.

---

27 'How to fill in job application forms and when to apply', *Dataquest*, 29 March 2019, https://www.dataquest.io/blog/career-guide-data-science-application-forms/

Following up on a job application

If you haven't heard anything from a company for a week or two you can follow up by phone or email. Normally, following up will not help your application, however in rare cases showing interest can result in an interview invitation.

Job application feedback

You can seek feedback on an unsuccessful job application where you weren't offered an interview, however the usual response will be that there were many experienced applicants. Because you're unlikely to get any valuable feedback, there's not much point asking. If you're not getting invited to any interviews then get feedback on your applications (resume, cover letters, and selection criteria responses) from a career counsellor or a friend who works in HR or recruiting.

Job applications key points

- Apply for jobs well before the closing date as some companies start interviewing before the closing date.

- Read the job application form and instructions, and answer questions in a separate document before copying your answers to the job application form.

- Don't provide any salary information. Where completing the salary field is mandatory, write '0' and elsewhere state that salary is negotiable.

- Don't seek feedback on an unsuccessful job application where you weren't offered an interview because you're unlikely to get any valuable feedback.

- If you're not getting any interviews, get feedback on your applications (resume, cover letters, and selection criteria responses) from a career counsellor or a friend who works in HR or recruiting.

Accessing the hidden job market

The hidden job market is defined as vacant jobs which are not advertised.

Approximately 19% of all jobs are never advertised.[28] Why? When an employee leaves a company or a new job is created, the company wants to fill the vacancy as quickly as possible. It costs money to advertise a job and time to recruit an employee. If a company can find an employee without having to spend money on advertising and time recruiting, they will. Eliminating the time spent advertising and waiting for job applications to be received will result in the vacancy being filled faster.

How hidden job market jobs are filled

- Someone working in the company knows someone who needs a job.
- A manager asks team members if they know someone to fill a vacancy.

---

[28] Australian Government, National Skills Commission, *Survey of employers' recruitment experiences: 2019 data report*, https://lmip.gov.au/PortalFile.axd?FieldID=3193776&.pdf

- Headhunting: an employer asks someone they know if they would like a job.

- Reverse marketing: a recruiter with a suitable job seeker contacts a company on the off-chance they have a vacancy that they have not yet advertised.

- A job seeker contacts a company directly to offer their skills.

- An employer searches LinkedIn for people with the qualification and experience they need.

When you need a plumber, for example, you usually don't get one from the internet or an ad in a local newspaper; you ask someone for a recommendation. People prefer to get a recommended plumber rather than have someone they don't know. It's the same with employers hiring employees.

Some companies have a referral bonus scheme where an employee is paid for recommending a person who is subsequently hired and successfully completes a probationary period.

Accessing hidden market jobs

You can access hidden job market jobs in a number of different ways:

- Networking with people
    - family
    - friends
    - colleagues (via LinkedIn)
    - professional associations/alumni associations.

- Directly approaching employers
  - marketing email/LinkedIn
  - phone calls
  - door knocking
  - recommendations from employees.

Networking with people

Start by networking with family, friends, and former colleagues. While you may not feel like telling people that you are out of work or asking for assistance, people are usually happy to assist when they can. Let people know that you are looking for work in your field. Sometimes, family, friends, or former colleagues will know of a job opportunity or potential job opportunity for you. They may know of a worker or manager in your field and can introduce you to that person.

Connect with former colleagues through LinkedIn (see the chapter 'LinkedIn as a job search tool') and meet with them for coffee. When one person you have contacted lets you know of an opportunity, you should speak directly to their contact rather than letting your contact speak on your behalf. Ensure you are the person who sends your resume to the contact. Don't lose control of your resume by giving it to people you know to pass on to their contacts.

Join a professional association/alumni association and attend their professional development events. Join their social media group if they have one and contribute to the discussions. Connect with members of the professional association/alumni association through LinkedIn (see the chapter 'LinkedIn as a job search tool').

Keep your contacts updated on the status of your job search.

Directly approaching employers

Why should you approach employers who are not currently advertising a job in your field? Because they may need someone in the short to medium term and, if they already know you, they may employ you to save time and money advertising. For 11% of vacancies, employers consider people who have approached them looking for work, with many employers actually hiring them.[29] Also, employers may know of job vacancies in your field at other companies.

You may think that approaching employers when job searching is a sign of desperation, however employers view it as displaying initiative.

Contacting employers who are not currently advertising jobs is scary for most people, except perhaps salespeople. You are likely to be nervous and make some mistakes when you start contacting them. Hence, it is best to first approach a company that is not at the top of your list of companies you want to work for. Start with the 15th or 20th company you would like to work for. Once you have experience approaching companies then approach the companies you most want to work for.

To identify companies in which you are interested:

- ask for recommendations from family, friends, and colleagues
- google companies in your industry and location
- google competitors of <company name>

---

29 Australian Government, National Skills Commission, *Australian jobs 2020*, https://www.nationalskillscommission.gov.au/sites/default/files/2020-11/Australian%20Jobs%20Report%202020.pdf

- use LinkedIn (see the chapter 'LinkedIn as a job search tool')
- search business databases, some of which may be accessed free of charge at your local library or state library. Library members may be able to access a business database from home.

How to use a business database to find companies in your industry

As an example, if you worked for a confectionary company as a factory worker and seek a similar job, you can use a business database to list confectionary companies in your area by searching using the industry code for confectionary companies. Industry codes may be found in a list of standard industry classification codes. The Australian and New Zealand Standard Industrial Classification (ANZSIC) is one example. You can use the postcode or area code to list companies in your location.

Note that some jobs are industry specific, e.g. teachers working in schools. Other jobs are found in all industries, e.g. receptionists, analyst/programmers, and call centre operators. For a job found in all industries, you could search based on an industry you would like to work in or one you have worked in.

What's the best way to contact employers?

When you have a list of companies you are going to approach for work, how should you contact them? Is it best to make a phone call, send a marketing email, or cold canvas (drop into their workplace unannounced)? If you decide to send a marketing email, do you attach your resume? The answers depend on several factors.

Dropping off a resume in person to an employer

Only drop off a resume in person for an advertised job when instructed to do so. You can drop off a resume to access the hidden job market. Dropping off a resume in person to access the hidden job market used to be common, however many companies will now only accept resumes through the careers page of their website.

Dropping off a resume in person is more likely to be successful at small businesses. When dropping off a resume, ensure you are well dressed and groomed. Attend the business when they are not too busy. A bad time to attend a restaurant or fast-food shop is just prior to or during mealtimes. Be polite and friendly to all the staff. Say you are there to drop off your resume and ask to speak with the manager. If the manager or a hiring decision maker is not there, ask what day or time you can come back to give them your resume in person. If they insist on taking your resume to pass to the manager, ask for the manager's name and phone number to touch base with them in a few days. Most people who drop off resumes make the mistake of never going back to the business. Keep in touch by contacting management on a regular agreed basis. If the manager is there, don't just hand them your resume and leave. Engage the manager with some conversation about their business.

Phoning an employer

Phoning an employer works well with small companies that don't have HR staff and where it is possible to speak with the person making hiring decisions, i.e. the hiring manager. It can be a successful way of finding relatively easy to get jobs like cleaning, water meter reading, and entry-level jobs.

Why you need to speak with the hiring manager

Phoning larger companies is problematic due to the high likelihood of being transferred to HR after the receptionist finds out you want a job. Many receptionists act as gatekeepers to protect management from phone queries. You want to speak with the hiring manager rather than HR.

The reasons for avoiding HR are that they:

- may not yet know of an impending vacancy
- tend to be risk averse and will not pass resumes on to the hiring manager
- are busy with other work
- do not have the authority to hire a job seeker
- may not realise that the job seeker's background matches a need in their company.

Experienced employment consultants and job search books agree that avoiding HR is the best strategy (Levinson and Perry, 2005; Cohen 2001).[30] If you end up in a situation where you phone a company and the receptionist offers to put your call through to HR, politely decline and send a marketing email to the hiring manager. This is because HR will ask you to email them your

---

30 JC Levinson and DE Perry 2005, *Guerrilla marketing for job hunters*, John Wiley & Sons Inc., Hoboken, New Jersey; WA Cohen 2001, *Break the rules: the secret code to finding a great job fast*, Prentice Hall Press Books., Harlow, United Kingdom

resume and you will likely never again hear from that company. The hiring manager knows the company's hiring needs and is the decision maker.

How to find out the name of the hiring manager

You may find out the name of the hiring manager by:

- searching LinkedIn (see the chapter 'LinkedIn as a job search tool')
- browsing the company website
- searching a business database.

If you're not sure whom to contact, one option is to contact the most senior person in a small company or a general or senior manager in a mid-sized/large company. If you contact someone senior, they may delegate their subordinate manager to contact you. This can work out well as the subordinate manager will be obliged to meet with you. If, instead, you contact the subordinate manager directly, they may not take the time to meet with you, especially if they're busy.

Contacting a hiring manager by phone

The best time to phone the hiring manager is ideally at a time when they are open but not busy. This will vary depending on the type of business. When you phone you can always ask the hiring manager if they have a moment to talk. If they say no, then arrange a time to call back or leave a message for them to call you back. If you leave a message, give your name and phone number. Don't say you're wanting a job as they will be less likely to return your call.

What to say when you phone

Hiring manager: Hello, Jane speaking.

Job seeker: Hello, my name is John Smith. I'm looking for cleaning work. Do you have any?

Two responses are possible.

Response 1

Hiring manager: Yes. We have a job available. Could you send your resume?

Job seeker: Yes. What is your email address?

Hiring manager: My email address is ....

Job seeker: Thanks. I'll send it now.

Hiring manager: Thanks.

Job seeker: Bye.

Hiring manager: Bye.

Response 2

Hiring manager: No. We're right for staff.

Job seeker: Is there any work coming up in the future?

In this scenario, two further responses are possible:

Response 2A

Hiring manager: We may need someone in the next few months.

Job seeker:	I've got two years' cleaning experience.
Hiring manager:	Can you send me your resume? We are always on the lookout for good staff.
Job seeker:	Yes. I can email it to you. What's your email address?
Hiring manager:	My email address is ....
Job seeker:	Thanks. I'll send it now. Is it okay if I keep in contact with you?
Hiring manager:	You can phone me monthly.
Job seeker:	Thanks. Bye.
Hiring manager:	Bye.

Response 2B

Hiring manager:	No.
Job seeker:	Do you know of anyone who may be able to help me?
Hiring manager:	You might try XYZ Company. The manager's name is ....
Job seeker:	Thanks. Is it okay if I mention your name when I call the XYZ manager?
Hiring manager:	Yes. Good luck.
Job seeker:	Thanks. Bye.
Hiring manager:	Bye.

The job seeker should phone the hiring manager on an agreed regular basis to keep their name uppermost in the hiring manager's mind. This way, when they need to hire, they are likely to think of the job seeker who has kept in contact regularly rather than advertise or hire someone else.

Contacting a hiring manager by email

A marketing email works well for middle-sized and larger companies. Send a marketing email to the hiring manager. Refer to Appendix G for a marketing email template. Refer to Appendices H and I for examples of marketing emails. Appendix H is an example of a marketing email for someone who is not changing fields. Appendix I is an example of a marketing email for someone who is changing fields.

Another option is to send a marketing letter by post. The advantages of sending a marketing letter are that:

- the hiring manager receives few letters but many emails
- it is more difficult for the hiring manager to bin a letter than delete an email.

The advantage of sending a marketing email is that it is cheaper and faster than a marketing letter.

How to find out the hiring manager's email address

You will need to guess the format of the hiring manager's username which is before the @ character. For example, you could try john.smith, jsmith, john_smith, etc. Look at the company website for the email domain, i.e. the part of the address after the @ character. Send the email with different name formats until the email doesn't bounce back to you unsent, i.e. it has been successfully delivered.

A couple of days after sending the marketing email, phone the hiring manager to whom you addressed your email.

How to bypass the gatekeeper receptionist when you phone

When the receptionist answers the phone and asks why you want to speak with the hiring manager, say you are following up on an email you sent them.

If the hiring manager doesn't answer their phone, leave a message on their answering machine saying that you are following up on the email you sent and ask that they return your call.

If the hiring manager answers the phone, you can ask them to meet with you for a short time to gain their thoughts and ideas about the industry. Don't ask if they have any vacancies because they will likely say that they are not currently hiring and that will end the phone call and your chance of a face-to-face meeting. This type of face-to-face meeting is known as an informational interview.

Informational interviews

Informational interviews enable you to:

- meet hiring managers
- ask hiring managers questions about their industry
- find job opportunities in the hiring manager's industry.

An informational interview is different to a job interview in that the job seeker asks the questions. Before approaching the employer for an informational interview, research the industry in which you want to work. You need to know the largest companies, industry trends, and jargon.

Informational interview objectives

The aim of an informational interview:

- Get information about:
    - the industry
    - a company's needs/problems
    - the hiring manager's career background.
- Get advice on:
    - how to utilise your background in their industry.
- Get referrals to other hiring managers and industry contacts to:
    - uncover a hidden job.
- Help your contact (hiring manager) by:
    - sharing information on an industry
    - listening
    - sharing ideas.
- The value of an informational interview:
    - depends on the hiring manager

- depends on how closely your background matches their future employment needs
- may be low when it is scheduled to avoid offending you.

Questions to ask at an informational interview

Google 'informational interview questions' so you know what questions to ask at these interviews.

For example:

- What sort of qualifications/background do people need to work in the industry?
- What does a typical workday look like?
- Are my qualifications/background a good fit for this industry?
- Which companies are hiring at present?
- Which companies are the major players in this industry?
- What salary could I expect to receive?
- What growth/training opportunities are there?

If the informational interview goes well, you could ask the hiring manager the following questions:

- Is it okay to keep in touch with you?
- How often should I contact you?
- Is phone or email preferable?
- Do you know of any people in the industry who may be able to assist me?

- Is it okay if I mention your name when contacting them?

When you keep in touch with them, don't ask if they have a job vacancy. Instead, give them information about the industry. If you find an interesting article, mention it to them.

If they agree that you can mention their name when you call the hiring manager's contact, the conversation may go like this:

> Job seeker: Hello, Joe. Heather (the hiring manager) gave me your name and suggested you may be able to assist me. I'm a receptionist currently researching the medical reception industry and hope that we could meet briefly to chat about the industry.

Joe is likely to accept your request to meet because he won't want to risk damaging his relationship with Heather. There is no need to get past the receptionist gatekeeper by sending a marketing email to Joe because you tell Joe's receptionist that Heather asked you to call Joe. Alternatively, you can send an email to Joe, mentioning Heather's name, if you feel more comfortable explaining what you want in an email rather than in a phone call.

A warm call is with someone you or your contact knows. It is more likely to be successful than a cold call, i.e. the phone call to Heather.

If the hiring manager asks you for a resume at an informational interview, don't immediately give it to them because you will have blown your cover reason for the meeting, which is to learn about the industry rather than ask for a job. If asked for your resume, say you are still researching the industry but will write a resume for them.

After the informational interview, send the hiring manager a thank you email thanking them for their time and views on the industry.

If you make a good impression with the hiring manager, then when they are looking for staff, perhaps in a few months' time, they will remember you and ask you for an interview to save themselves the time and cost involved in hiring through advertising. At that interview you may have little or no competition for the job.

The reason for sending a marketing email and not your resume is twofold:

1. You want to give the impression you are genuinely researching the industry to get a face-to-face informational interview and are not just asking for a job.
2. The information gained at an informational interview can be used to tailor your resume if the hiring manager asks you to provide a resume.

If you send an employer an email asking for work with a resume attached, instead of a marketing email, then when you phone the hiring manager, they will tell you there are no vacancies at present and may end the call. You're less likely to get the opportunity of making a good impression at a face-to-face meeting.

Elevator speech

Prepare an elevator speech to use when phoning a hiring manager. An elevator speech is what you would say to someone you meet going up or down in an elevator who asks what you do for a living. It should be 30 to 60 seconds long.

For example:

> I recently graduated from college with a degree in communications. I worked on the college newspaper as a reporter and, eventually, as the editor of the arts section. I'm looking for a job that will put my skills as a journalist to work.[31]

Do all organisations have hidden market jobs?

Some organisations such as governments, hospitals, and universities are required to advertise their jobs. For these organisations, networking may be of limited use as they don't have hidden market jobs. Having said this, some of these organisations may hire temporary staff without going through a formal recruitment process.

Consider being a boomerang employee

If you left a previous job on good terms, it's worth getting in touch with former co-workers to see whether there are new opportunities available. You won't need as much time for onboarding, are already familiar with the company's technology and culture, and can often contribute much more quickly.[32]

---

31 A Doyle, 'How to create an elevator pitch with examples', *The Balance Careers*, 27 January 2021, https://www.thebalancecareers.com/elevator-speech-examples-and-writing-tips-2061976
32 R Hein and S Florentine, '10 tips for job hunting while you're still employed', *CIO Australia*, 13 August 2019, https://www.cio.com/article/2387929/careers-staffing-8-tips-for-job-hunting-while-you-re-still-employed.html

Accessing the hidden job market key points

- Approximately 19% of jobs are not advertised.[33]
- Contact the hiring manager of a potential employer rather than HR.
- To get past the receptionist, email the hiring manager with your marketing email. Follow up with a phone call to schedule an informational interview.
- An informational interview is a face-to-face meeting with a potential employer who is not currently advertising.
- Informational interviews with hiring managers enable a job seeker to make a good impression, learn about the industry, and hopefully keep in contact with the employer for when a vacancy does occur.

---

33 Australian Government, National Skills Commission, *Survey of employers' recruitment experiences: 2019 data report*, https://lmip.gov.au/PortalFile.axd?FieldID=3193776&.pdf

Job search strategy

Using more than one method of job seeking will help you find work more quickly.

Some job seekers apply for a large number of jobs advertised online with little success. Rather than a 'shotgun' approach, i.e. indiscriminate and haphazard, a more targeted approach applying for jobs that you have a good chance of getting may be more fruitful.

Most job seekers only apply for advertised jobs and don't search for unadvertised or hidden market jobs. There are two problems with this strategy:

1. Large numbers of job seekers are doing the same thing, so there is a lot of competition and hence only a small chance of success.

2. Job seekers are missing out on jobs that are not advertised, which is around 19% of all jobs.[34]

Therefore, 19% of time spent job seeking should be spent searching for jobs that are not advertised, i.e. the hidden market jobs. Because fewer job seekers access the hidden job market,

---

[34] Australian Government, National Skills Commission, *Survey of employers' recruitment experiences: 2019 data report*, https://lmip.gov.au/PortalFile.axd?FieldID=3193776&.pdf

those who do have a larger chance of obtaining hidden market jobs than advertised jobs. So, you might decide to spend more than 19% of your job seeking time accessing the hidden job market due to the larger chance of obtaining those jobs.

If replying to online job ads is a part of your job search strategy, then google 'websites to use for job seeking' and 'niche job board list' to ensure that the websites you use are the best for the type of work you are looking for.

Register for job alerts on job boards to receive emails of jobs advertised that interest you. Job alerts can be set up for jobs with a specific job title and for a classification/industry so as not to miss out on jobs with unusual job titles. For example, a person who registers a job alert for 'career counsellor' will miss a job titled 'Industry Liaison Officer' unless an alert is set up to include all jobs in the 'Education' classification.

Deciding where to spend your job seeking time based on Labour Market Information

It is useful to review labour market information when planning your targeted job search strategy. See the chapter 'Labour market information'. An Australian Government report outlines industry and occupation data such as the following, which may influence your decision as to where you spend your job seeking time.

Recruitment methods differ significantly by industry [and occupation]. Recruitment websites and job boards were the most commonly used recruitment method in all industries, but this ranged from 63% of employers in education and training to 37% of employers in accommodation and food services. Word of mouth was most commonly used in transport, postal and warehousing (where it was used by 36% of recruiting employers), wholesale trade (33%) and construction (33%). One in five businesses recruiting in the manufacturing industry used recruitment agencies or employment services providers. Direct approaches by job seekers were most commonly used for recruitment in retail trade (13%), accommodation and food services (11%) and transport, postal and warehousing (10%).[35]

Recruitment websites and job boards were also the most commonly used recruitment method for each occupation, however their usage varied from 62% of employers recruiting for managers to 35% of employers recruiting for labourers. The use of word of mouth was less common in recruitment for professionals (21% of recruiting employers), and was highest in recruitment for labourers (31%). Recruitment agencies and employment services providers were most commonly used by employers recruiting for labourers (19%). Employers recruiting sales workers were the most likely to use a company website (19%), direct approaches from job seekers (12%) or a sign in a business window (11%).[36]

A breakdown of occupations and industries where employers did not advertise when recruiting because they used 'word of mouth', job seekers approached them, and/or the employer approached the job seekers is in 'Appendix K: Percentage of recruiting employers who did not advertise by occupation', and 'Appendix L: Percentage of recruiting employers who did not advertise by industry'.

---

[35] Australian Government, National Skills Commission, *Employers' insights on the Australian labour market: 2020 data report*, pp. 37–38, https://lmip.gov.au/default.aspx?LMIP/GainInsights/EmployersRecruitmentInsights

[36] Australian Government, National Skills Commission, *Employers' insights on the Australian labour market: 2020 data report*, pp. 37–38

Job search intervention

The odds of getting a job are 2.67 times higher for a person who engages in a job search intervention, e.g. advice from a career counsellor, than a person who does not. The odds of success are higher for interventions that target proactivity, goals setting and enlisting social support.

The career development skills most effective in improving job search success are teaching job search skills, improving self-presentation, boosting self-efficacy, encouraging proactivity, promoting goal setting, and enlisting social support.[37]

Should you upload your resume to a job board/employer employment register?

When you upload your resume to a job board:

- you lose the opportunity to tailor it to a job ad
- you make your job search public
- employers and recruiters might headhunt you for a vacancy.

In any case, an employer or recruiter can search and find your LinkedIn profile, which has superseded uploading your resume to a job board.

---

[37] Career Development Association of Australia, *Career Development Works*, p. 12, https://cdaa.imiscloud.com/common/Uploaded%20files/About%20Career%20Development/CDAA%20Career%20Development%20Works.pdf

Many organisations not only list job vacancies on their website but also allow job seekers to upload their resumes to an employment register in case suitable job vacancies occur. The advantage of uploading your details is that you may be contacted for an interview. The disadvantage is that you cannot tailor your application to an advertised position. The exception is where jobs are advertised without closing dates as a company may regularly need these vacancies filled.

If your job search strategy is unsuccessful, you need to consider what changes to make to your strategy. This might include the following strategies:

- Apply for different types of jobs (some job seekers apply for jobs for which they are not qualified or experienced enough to get).
- Spend more time accessing the hidden job market by networking with family, friends, and colleagues, attending professional association and alumni activities, and by directly contacting employers.
- Get someone (preferably a HR professional/recruiter friend/career counsellor) to review your resume, cover letters, and selection criteria responses, especially if you are not getting any interviews.
- Research how to prepare for interviews if you are getting interviews but not being offered any jobs.
- Consider applying for part-time jobs even though you prefer full-time.
- Ask a career counsellor for assistance.

Job search strategy key points

- Most job seekers only apply for advertised jobs and don't search for unadvertised or hidden market jobs.

- As fewer job seekers access the hidden job market, those who do have a larger chance of obtaining hidden market jobs.

- Using more than one method of job seeking will help you find work more quickly.

- Many organisations not only list job vacancies on their website but also allow job seekers to upload their resumes to an employment register in case suitable job vacancies occur.

- Register for job alerts on job boards to receive emails for jobs advertised in your area of interest.

- If your job search strategy is unsuccessful, you need to consider what changes to make to your strategy.

LinkedIn as a job search tool

LinkedIn allows a person to create an online profile consisting of their employment history and educational background. It enables networking between people.

If you don't have a LinkedIn profile, now is the time to create one.

Privacy concerns

Google 'how to protect my privacy on LinkedIn' to learn ways in which you can protect and maintain your personal details on LinkedIn. Weigh the benefits of LinkedIn against your privacy concerns to decide whether/how to use LinkedIn. If you have privacy concerns, ensure you review all options in the 'Settings & Privacy' page (under your account profile) to see what you can do to protect your privacy.

If you are working while job searching, you need to be discreet in your job search activities so your current employer doesn't find out. The following steps will help to ensure your job search is undiscovered:

- Ensure that any profile edits you make are not shared with your network. Select 'Settings & Privacy' under your account profile, then choose 'Visibility'. Here you have the option to not share profile updates with your network.

- Don't post any LinkedIn status updates that would imply you are dissatisfied with your current job and/or looking for a new job opportunity.

- Don't post anything openly related to your job search in LinkedIn Groups, especially job search-oriented LinkedIn Groups.

- Don't show all of your groups on your profile. When joining LinkedIn groups related to job searching or any groups you don't want people from your current employer to see, go immediately to the group after joining. In the group settings you can choose not to display the group on your profile.

- Don't ask your current manager or colleagues for LinkedIn recommendations.

- On your profile page, ensure your public profile is fully visible to potential employers by turning on 'Your profile's public visibility' and choosing public for your profile photo.

- If you're viewing your current co-workers' profiles to see how they look, you might want to make yourself show up anonymous; however, if you are looking up recruiters or managers at target companies, you may want to make yourself show up with full information to prompt them to look at your profile. This can be achieved in the 'Visibility' page under 'Settings & Privacy'. Under profile viewing options you can choose for your name and

- Don't include your work contact information in your LinkedIn profile.
- Don't make your work email address the primary address on your LinkedIn account. If you do, messages and job opportunities sent via LinkedIn will end up in your inbox at work.[38]

headline to be fully represented or select private mode to be totally anonymous.

Starting to use LinkedIn

Learn how to use LinkedIn by reading the resources in LinkedIn Help. Google 'how to create a good LinkedIn profile' to write a compelling profile. Your profile can be longer and written in a less formal style than your resume. Include your photo in your profile unless you are concerned about age-based discrimination. Google 'how to take and choose a suitable professional photo for LinkedIn'. Ensure that your LinkedIn employment history matches that in your resume in case employers check they match. If you decide to include your pronouns in your profile, add them after your last name (see the 'Pronouns' section in the chapter 'Resume writing' for further information).

Ask former managers and colleagues to give you recommendations and endorse your skills. Join your professional association group and contribute to the discussion. Always send a message to a person whom you want to connect with. Don't initially say you are looking for work. After they connect with you then you can let them know you

---

38 T Storani, 'How to actually job search on LinkedIn in secret', 3 September 2018, https://www.linkedin.com/pulse/how-job-search-linkedin-secret-tana-storani/

are job hunting. Use the LinkedIn status update feature to let your connections know you are job hunting. Provide your email and phone number to make it easy for people to contact you. Consider posting articles and/or videos to build your profile.

When you have a good LinkedIn profile, you may want to include a link to your profile in the contact details section of your resume. It's a good idea to customise your LinkedIn URL to something meaningful like your name. Google 'how to customise your LinkedIn URL'.

In the chapter 'Resume writing', the section 'How many resumes do you need?' recommends a different resume for each type of job or occupation for which you apply, however LinkedIn does not support this as it allows only one profile per person. If you are in the situation where you are applying for two different types of jobs or occupations, choose one for your Headline and Summary for clarity or alternatively include both and accept the risk of confusion in readers' minds.

How LinkedIn can assist your job search

Google 'how to search for companies on LinkedIn' and 'how to search LinkedIn by industry' to find companies and industries you want to target in your job search. Follow companies that you are interested in because companies post articles about their activities and post job ads. Google 'how to follow companies on LinkedIn'.

You can search for jobs that are advertised on LinkedIn and set up job alerts to be emailed jobs that meet your search criteria.

Read your interviewers' profiles before attending the interview.

Applying for jobs advertised on LinkedIn using 'Easy Apply' or 'Apply'

Job ads on LinkedIn have either an 'Easy Apply' or an 'Apply' button, chosen by the advertiser. 'Easy Apply' forwards details of your LinkedIn profile to the advertiser. 'Apply' directs you to the company's website or job board to continue the application process.

When to use 'Easy Apply'

Use 'Easy Apply' when:

- your LinkedIn profile is up to date and complete
- your LinkedIn profile is an excellent match for the job
- you don't have the time to complete a traditional job application
- you are not making a career change
- the job is not your dream job.

'Easy Apply' does include an option to attach a tailored resume to your application, however an employer/recruiter will initially only see your LinkedIn profile and may not browse your resume.

Search Engine Optimisation

To increase your profile position in search results, refer to the LinkedIn article '11 SEO tips for your personal LinkedIn profile'.[39]

---

39 B Shumway, '11 SEO tips for your personal LinkedIn profile', 20 March 2014, https://www.linkedin.com/pulse/20140320151331-142790335-11-seo-tips-for-your-personal-linkedin-profile

Networking using LinkedIn

LinkedIn enables networking in a number of different ways:

- Search for people to connect and network with. For example, searching for a tax lawyer provides a list of people who have tax lawyer in their Headline field.

- Search for fellow alumni by searching for the university/college you attended and filtering the search by qualification and course completion date.

- Connect and network with members of your professional association group.

- Connect with colleagues/lecturers/tutors/team leaders/managers.

- Connect with people who you think may be helpful in your job search.

- Search for recruiters in your field and location and connect with them. Include a short message introducing yourself and attach your resume. Read the LinkedIn article, 'How to find recruiters on LinkedIn'.[40]

- Network with your connections who work in companies you'd like to work for.

- If one of your connections has a connection who works in a company you'd like to work for, ask your connection to introduce you to their connection. Google 'how to ask for a LinkedIn introduction'.

---

[40] D Boggs, 'How to find recruiters on LinkedIn', 24 October 2019, https://www.linkedin.com/pulse/how-find-recruiters-linkedin-debra-boggs-msm/

- If you're applying for a job, connect with employees of that company and ask to be recommended because many companies have a bonus scheme where employees receive a bonus for recommending a person who is subsequently hired. Ensure you're recommended before sending off the job application so your connection is eligible for their bonus.

LinkedIn headline

In their LinkedIn headline, people who are unemployed should write, e.g. 'Tax Lawyer seeking a new opportunity' rather than 'Unemployed seeking work', as recruiters/employers searching LinkedIn for a tax lawyer will see your profile in their search results.

Should you subscribe to LinkedIn premium?

Consider subscribing to LinkedIn premium. Google the pros and cons of subscribing.

LinkedIn as a job search tool key points

- Join LinkedIn and create a profile.

- Privacy concerns can be managed via the 'Settings & Privacy' page.

- Improve you profile position in search results using SEO.

- If you are not currently working, write a headline with your desired occupation/job title stating you're looking for an opportunity.

- Connect and network with colleagues, fellow alumni, and members of your professional association.

- Set up job alerts to be emailed jobs advertised on LinkedIn that meet your criteria.

- You can apply for jobs on LinkedIn using 'Easy Apply' or 'Apply'.

Using a recruitment agency

Recruitment agencies are businesses that are paid to find suitable workers for other companies.[41] Recruiters who work at these agencies achieve their key performance indicators (KPIs) by placing suitable job seekers with an employer, thereby making money for their company. Recruiters are not working to find a job for every job seeker who registers with them.

About 15% of vacancies are filled through an employment agency, such as a private recruitment agency, labour hire firm, or Australian Government funded employment services provider.[42]

How to choose a recruitment agency

Search LinkedIn for recruiters in your field and location, and contact them via LinkedIn. See the chapter 'LinkedIn as a job search tool'. If you are looking for work as an accountant, for example, and 100–200 job seekers apply for each advertised job,

---

41 *Cambridge Dictionary*, https://dictionary.cambridge.org/dictionary/english/recruitment-agency (amended)
42 Australian Government, Department of Employment, 'Recruitment methods used by employers', 18 May 2017, https://www.dese.gov.au/employment-research-and-statistics/resources/recruitment-methods-used-employers-0

then you won't get much attention from a recruiter. However, if your employment and training background is unique or rare, then a recruiter may respond to you reaching out to them via LinkedIn. To get a list of recruitment agencies who specialise in the area in which you are job searching, see how many ads each agency is placing to determine which are the busiest. Google recruitment agencies that operate in your field of work.

Get a colleague who has been a recruiter's job seeker to refer you to the recruiter. Ask the colleague to let the recruiter know that you will call them.

If you can, connect with about five recruitment companies. Working with a larger number of recruiters may not be more helpful for your job prospects. For example, working with 15 or 50 recruitment companies where none of them are putting you forward for work is not a good use of your time. If they are putting you forward to employers, working with a smaller number of recruitment companies will likely be all that you need.

Managing a relationship with a recruiter

Be polite and respectful to the recruiter. Inform the recruiter what it is you want and don't want in a job. Keep in touch with a recruiter if they ask you to. Each time you call the recruiter don't just ask if they have any jobs; instead, give them general but not specific information about how you think the job market is currently trending in your field. You might say, 'There seem to be more ads in the last two weeks.'

Don't say to one recruiter that you are, for example, a chief financial officer but if you cannot find work you would work as an accountant, and if you cannot find accounting work you would work as a bookkeeper. While this example is a little farfetched, you don't want to send a negative message to the recruiter. If you are looking for work in, say, three occupations, use three recruiters, one for each occupation. In such a situation you would need to tailor your resume for each recruiter. See the chapter 'Resume writing'.

One question a job seeker should ask when they see a job ad placed by a recruiter is 'Is this a real job?' Sometimes an employer will say to a recruiter that they may need a couple of project managers, for example, in a month. So, the recruiter places an ad and interviews job seekers to have suitable job seekers ready should the employer be ready to hire. However, the positions may be filled internally within the company or the projects may be cancelled or deferred.

At an interview with a recruiter, you can ask how often they place a person with your experience in a job.

It is worthwhile contacting a recruiter who has not advertised a job in your field, however the level of interest a recruiter has in you will depend on whether they think they can place you in a job. A recruiter may try to reverse market you into a company that currently has no vacancy by sending your resume to the hiring manager.

When you speak by phone with a recruiter who asks you to email them a resume, they may just be trying to end the phone call rather than displaying a real interest in you. A recruiter's interest in you can rapidly change if an employer asks them to fill a vacancy where you would be a suitable person.

A survey[43] found that only 26% of recruiters consider cover letters important in their decision to hire an applicant, so when applying for jobs advertised by recruiters, only attach your resume. Unless specifically requested, don't go to the trouble of writing a cover letter.

Sometimes a recruiter will suggest you make changes to your resume. While you may have spent a lot of time writing your resume, comply with their request. You can decide if you want to change your resume master copy.

At an interview with a recruiter, which can occur either by phone, video conferencing, or in person, they may ask why you left each of your jobs and what you did in each job. Be prepared with answers. Asking the recruiter a couple of good questions can help to build a relationship with them. See the chapters 'Face-to-face and video interviews' and 'Phone screening interviews' to prepare for interviews with recruiters.

If a recruiter asks which companies you have interviewed with, don't tell them because they might try to put forward job seekers to those companies if the jobs haven't been filled. They may be trying to ascertain how much you are in demand.

Ask the recruiter if they only work with job seekers or if they also work with employers. Rarely, but sometimes, a recruiter only works with job seekers and another recruiter in the agency will work with employers. If that's the case, ask to meet with the recruiter who works with employers so they will be able to put

---

43 Jobvite, *2017 Job seeker nation study: finding the fault lines in the American workforce*, p.19, https://www.jobvite.com/wp-content/uploads/2017/05/2017_Job_Seeker_Nation_Survey.pdf

a name to a face and 'sell' you more confidently to an employer after having met you.

A recruiter may only be interviewing you to meet a KPI to interview a certain number of people per week and may not actually have a job suitable for you.

At the end of an interview with a recruiter, you can ask if they feel comfortable putting you forward to an employer.

Ethical recruiters will only put your resume forward after asking you for permission. You may wish to google 'recruiters' tricks' to learn about some less than savoury tactics used.

If recruiters are not putting you forward to employers, then at least you are only missing out on less than 15% of the available job vacancies.[44]

Salary discussion with a recruiter

Recruiters will ask your current salary or how much you were getting in your last job if you're not currently working. Their reason for asking about salary is that they don't want to waste their time putting you forward for a job that is not paying enough to satisfy your salary needs. However, don't tell them your current or your most recent salary as it shouldn't restrict how much you can get in your next job. Tell the recruiter that your current or most recent salary is confidential due to signing a contract where you agreed to not disclose your salary to anyone. They will ask

---

[44] Australian Government, Department of Employment, 'Recruitment methods used by employers', 18 May 2017, https://www.dese.gov.au/employment-research-and-statistics/resources/recruitment-methods-used-employers-0

you what salary you expect. Do your research beforehand so you know what the upper limit is for the job you're applying for. Don't give a salary range as the lower of the two figures may be used as your acceptable salary.

> ## Using a recruitment agency key points
>
> - Recruitment agencies comprise a small percentage of available jobs.
> - Introduce yourself to a few agencies that have jobs in your field.
> - Recruiters will only be interested in you if they think they can place you in a job.
> - 26% of recruiters consider cover letters important in their decision to hire an applicant so don't waste your time writing them unless the job ad specifically asks for a cover letter.[45]
> - Recruiters are paid by employers to fill vacancies with suitable job seekers.
> - Research salary for your level prior to speaking with the recruiter. Don't tell them your current or most recent salary.

---

45 Jobvite, *2017 Job seeker nation study: finding the fault lines in the American workforce*, p.19, https://www.jobvite.com/wp-content/uploads/2017/05/2017_Job_Seeker_Nation_Survey.pdf

Phone screening interviews

Phone interviews are often used by employers/recruiters for an initial screening to ensure the interviewees they advance to the hiring manager meet their minimum requirements.[46]

A screening interview includes a brief review of your educational and employment background and answering a few questions. The interviewer may also want to know your salary requirements and availability to work (whether or not you can start immediately).[47] The length of a phone screening interview is shorter than a face-to-face interview, usually about 15 to 30 minutes.

When they call, they will ask if you are free now to answer some questions. To allow yourself time to prepare for their questions say that you are busy right now and make a time for them to call you back. Conduct the phone interview somewhere quiet where you won't be disturbed.

---

46 '15 phone interview questions and answers', *Indeed Career Guide*, 5 February 2020, https://au.indeed.com/career-advice/interviewing/phone-interview-questions-and-answers

47 A Doyle, 'What is a screening interview?', *The Balance Careers*, updated 26 June 2020, https://www.thebalancecareers.com/what-is-a-screening-interview-2062094

Research the company by browsing their website. Make sure you can answer the following questions:

- What do you know about our company?
- Tell us about yourself?
- What is your understanding of the job?
- What interests you about the job?
- What are your strengths?
- Why are you leaving your current job?
- What salary would you like to earn in this job?
- What is your availability, i.e. when could you start in the new role?

Refer to the next chapter to learn how to answer interview questions.

To gain rapport, if the interviewer is talking slowly and is friendly, you can do the same. If they are talking fast and business-like, you can match them.

Ask the interviewer questions to indicate your interest in the job. You can google 'phone interview questions to ask the interviewer' to select suitable questions for your situation. Refer to the next chapter for more information on interviews.

Phone interview feedback

It is unlikely that you will be able to obtain worthwhile feedback from a phone interview because the interviewer is determining cultural fit and skillset.[48]

Phone screening interviews key points

- When you are contacted for a phone screening interview, say you are busy and make a time that will give you time to prepare.
- Prepare by developing answers to likely interview questions (covered in the next chapter).
- Be prepared to tell the interviewer about your relevant qualifications and experience.

---

48 J Petkanics, 'Tips from a recruiter: how to ask for feedback after a job rejection', *Brazen*, 25 September 2013, https://www.brazen.com/resources/tips-from-a-recruiter-how-to-ask-for-feedback-after-a-job-rejection

Face-to-face and video interviews

This chapter covers many scenarios of face-to-face interviews including video interviews, digital interviews, panel interviews, and group interviews. The general tips given are applicable in all scenarios.

Interview preparation

Prepare for an interview by researching likely interview questions and developing answers. Google 'interview questions and answers'. You could also google interview questions for your occupation.

Review the job ad, position description, and the company's website and social media profile and posts. Request a position description from the employer if they have not provided one.

When invited to the interview, ask the names and job titles of the interviewers. Memorise their names and browse their photos on LinkedIn so you can address them by name at the interview.

What to wear to an interview

As a rule, dress one level higher than the clothes you would wear each day if you were doing the job.

You can ask the person inviting you to the interview what the dress code is for the company.

If you're interviewing for a corporate position in finance or law, for example, wear formal business attire. For men, this means a matching suit and tie. For women, it means a tailored dress, pantsuit, or skirt suit. However, for less formal positions and workplaces, business casual is almost always the best option. Although it doesn't have a strict definition, business casual generally means dressing professionally without being overly formal. It's a step up from jeans and a t-shirt but a step down from formal business attire.

Avoid wearing:

- thongs and other open-toed sandals
- athletic shoes
- tank tops or shirts with thin straps
- shorts
- underwear that sticks out from your clothing
- skirts or dresses that are too short
- shirts with too-low necklines or that expose your belly
- perfume or cologne.[49]

---

[49] 'What to wear: the best job interview attire', *Indeed Career Guide*, 10 June 2021, https://www.indeed.com/career-advice/interviewing/what-to-wear-to-an-interview

Some organisations, for example, Fitted for Work, provide free work-appropriate clothing for job seekers experiencing disadvantage to attend interviews and start work.

Researching if a company is a good place to work

To determine if a company that has invited you to an interview is a good place to work, search LinkedIn using the company name to find out how long ex-employees worked there.

Browse the job search website Glassdoor where past and current employees review the companies they worked at.

Do some online research to find out if the company that is interviewing you is restructuring, losing money, or being sold. Read the article '50+ Google searches to avoid bad employers and pending layoffs' for different search queries to assist you with your research.[50]

Avoid companies:

- that ask you to perform unpaid work
- where the interviewer does not seem friendly.

Interview scheduling

Experts believe that there are two optimum periods for scheduling an interview: between 10am and 11am and between 2pm and

---

50 S Joyce, '50+ Google searches to avoid bad employers and pending layoffs', *Job-Hunt*, https://www.job-hunt.org/google-for-layoff-avoidance/

4pm. Researchers suggest that a morning interview might give you the edge over other interviewees.

While some studies found that it is better to attend an interview between Tuesday and Thursday, one study found Tuesday is the best day. Other studies suggest Friday may not be too detrimental to your chances, however all concur Monday is not a good day.[51]

You may not have a lot of choice when scheduling an interview depending on how many interview slots are left when you are contacted. If you are working, ask to be scheduled before or after work or during your lunch break. If this is not possible, ask to be interviewed by phone or video conferencing. While being interviewed by phone or video conferencing may put you at a disadvantage to people who are interviewed in person, it may be the only suitable arrangement for you.

What to do if you are sick when you have an interview

The best option is to phone the interviewer to say you're unwell, apologise for any inconvenience and ask for the interview to be rescheduled. Let them know that you don't want them to catch it from you. Give them a date by which time you will be well. Alternatively, the interviewer may agree to a video interview.

Likely interview questions

Question: Tell us about yourself.

---

[51] A Hoffarber, 'Is there really a best time to schedule an interview?', *Skywater blog, Skywater Search Partners*, 26 January 2019, https://blog.skywatersearch.com/is-there-really-a-best-time-to-schedule-an-interview

The reason many interviews start with this question is that most people find it easy to talk about themselves, which helps an interviewee to settle their nerves and feel more comfortable.

The employer does not want to know about your personal life.

Use the following structure to answer the question 'Tell us about yourself'.

- Present: Talk about your current role or situation.
- Past: Discuss your previous roles or experience, focusing on what's relevant to the role you're applying for.
- Future: Share your career goals and why this role would help you achieve them.[52]

Question: Name three of your strengths.

Consider the job ad and position description when deciding which strengths to include in your answer. For each strength, provide an example of where and how you used the strength and the result. You could use the STAR framework which is described in the chapter 'Key selection criteria'. Don't be too boastful or too humble.

For example:

> My greatest strength is my writing skills. I can also work to tight deadlines under pressure. For example, I was once asked to complete a project that fell through the cracks.

---

[52] 'How to answer: "So, tell me about yourself"', *Seek*, https://www.seek.com.au/career-advice/article/how-to-answer-so-tell-me-about-yourself

My editor discovered the mistake two hours before the deadline.

It was an important piece that gave our publication a scoop on the topic in question. Not only did the piece have to go out on time, but it had to be perfect. I hunkered down and wrote. The result? The article was on time and acclaimed.[53]

Question: Why do you want to work for us?

Possible answers:

- My skill set is very relevant to the job because ...
- I would appreciate the opportunity to work for a company that ...
- This job fits with my career plan, which is to ...

Don't say that you want to work for the company because they pay well or that you need a job.

Question: What is your weakness?

Sample answers:

- When I'm working on a project, I don't want just to meet deadlines. Rather, I prefer to complete the project well ahead of schedule.
- Being organised wasn't my strongest point, so I implemented a time management system that really helped my organisation skills.

---

53 N Severt, 'What are your strengths for an interview? [Greatest examples]', *Zety*, 7 July 2021, https://zety.com/blog/what-are-your-strengths

Responding that you don't have any weaknesses is a poor answer for two reasons:

1. Nobody's perfect. We all have strengths and weaknesses. The interviewers may think that you are either conceited or untruthful.
2. You miss the opportunity to say that you turned a weakness into a strength through actions you took.

Question: Why are you leaving your current job? Why did you leave your last job?

Be prepared to say why you left each job you've had. Never give an answer that is critical of your last employer. Never mention salary or interpersonal issues. It's fine to say that your position was made redundant, as it happens so often that it's no longer seen as a negative.

Give a positive answer such as wanting:

- a new challenge
- more responsibility
- experience not available at your previous employer.

Question: Why is there a gap in your resume/employment?

An employer/recruiter can see a gap in your resume/employment before they invite you to an interview. By inviting you to an interview they are not too concerned with any gaps.

You can explain gaps by saying you were:

- travelling

- unwell but have completely recovered
- made redundant
- caring for a relative but don't need to continue caring for them
- studying
- job searching with a view to finding a close match.

If you were fired/sacked from a job, it is better to say the work/job/contract ended. Another option is to admit you were sacked and say what you learned from being sacked.

Question: How do you handle stress?

Everybody gets stressed sometimes. The employer is interested in your awareness of your stress level and what you do to reduce it. In your answer, you might explain how stress motivates you to complete your work and give an example of how you have handled stress in a work situation. Don't choose an example that you caused. Don't say that you don't get stressed.

It may be that the employer is asking how you handle stress because the job is quite stressful. If you're wanting to work in a less stressful environment, then at the end of the interview you might ask about:

- work-life balance
- what a typical day looks like
- how the company views timelines
- how success is measured.

Based on the employer's answers, you may choose to work in a less stressful job.

Question: Where do you see yourself in five years?

When employers ask about where you want to be in five years, they're likely looking for a few key pieces of information:

- Do your expectations align with what the employer can provide?
- Do you see yourself at the company in five years?
- Do you have a sense of ambition or drive?
- What are your interests?

Do some prep-work before answering this question in an interview:

1. Think about how your goals fit with the job description.
2. Envision the experiences you'd like to have in your resume in five years.
3. Reflect on your interests and how they might evolve.

While not being specific can seem harmful in answering other interview questions, it is acceptable (and possibly helpful) to keep your answer to this question more general. Outlining a few key areas that you feel are interesting, achievable, and relevant to the role can provide sufficient information for the employer while also making your future seem flexible.[54]

---

54 'Interview question: "Where do you see yourself in five years?"', *Indeed Career Guide*, 5 February 2020, https://au.indeed.com/career-advice/interviewing/interview-question-where-do-you-see-yourself-in-five-years

Don't joke about how you'll be the one on the other side of the table in five years.[55]

Behavioural event interview (BEI) questions

A behavioural event interview (BEI) question is a type of interview question that is:

- focused on what you have done in the past
- based on the premise that past behaviour is the best predictor of future behaviour
- asking you to relate work history stories that link your experience and skills to the position.

For example:

- Tell me about a time when you provided excellent customer service.
- Please provide an example of a time where you have worked as part of an effective team, articulating your individual contribution.
- Describe a team project you worked on. What problems arose? How did you deal with them?
- Describe a situation when you had to persuade others to support your view.
- Give an example of a report you've written that illustrates your writing skills.

---

55 N Severt, 'How to best answer "Where do you see yourself in 5 years?" [Sample]', *Zety*, 19 February 2021, https://zety.com/blog/where-do-you-see-yourself-in-5-years

- Describe a time when you took responsibility to achieve a challenging goal.
- Tell us about a time when you had several tasks to manage at one time with conflicting deadlines.

Answering BEI questions

The STAR framework introduced in the 'Key selection criteria' chapter can assist you in answering BEI questions:

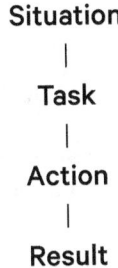

Situation
|
Task
|
Action
|
Result

Sample BEI question and answer

Question: Tell me about a time when you went above and beyond the requirements for a job.

Answer: When working as a Disability Employment Consultant at ABC company, my team leader told the whole office that I had completed a Graduate Diploma in Careers Education and Development. Staff in the office approached me, wanting to know how to assist their job seekers find suitable occupations. I decided to hold a workshop on the Holland Self-Directed Search career assessment tool and gained management approval to do so. The result was that 15 Employment Consultants in the office were skilled up in the use of a career assessment tool to assist their job seekers.

Analysing the above response using the STAR framework

- **Situation:** When working as a Disability Employment Consultant at ABC company, my team leader told the whole office that I had completed a Graduate Diploma in Careers Education and Development.

- **Task:** Staff in the office approached me, wanting to know how to assist their job seekers find suitable occupations.

- **Action:** I decided to hold a workshop on the Holland Self-Directed Search career assessment tool and gained management approval to do so.

- **Result:** The result was that 15 Employment Consultants in the office were skilled up in the use of a career assessment tool to assist their job seekers.

BEI questions relating to skills

Prepare for BEI questions relevant to your job covering the following skills:

- Ability to handle stress
- Problem solving
- Flexibility
- Customer focus
- Communication
- Initiative
- Decision making
- Goal setting

- Interpersonal skills
- Negotiation
- Teamwork
- Resilience
- Leadership (if you are applying for a job requiring leadership skills).

There are potentially dozens of BEI questions you might be asked in an interview, however if you prepare for about ten that cover relevant skills then that will be enough.

One likely BEI question:

- Have you ever had any problems working with a colleague and how did you manage the situation?

Interviewers are interested in hearing about your conflict management skills. Stick to scenarios where the conflict was resolved – people learned to work together – and an objective was successfully accomplished. Don't speak ill of anyone.[56] Don't tell the interviewer that you get along with everyone.[57] Highlight

---

56 'Describe a time when you got co-workers or classmates who dislike each other to work together. How did you accomplish this? What was the outcome?', *My Perfect Resume*, https://www.myperfectresume.com/career-center/interviews/questions/describe-a-time-where-you-mediated-between-two-colleagues

57 'Behavioral interview questions. Tell me about a time when you had to work with someone who was difficult to get along with', *Mock Questions*, https://www.mockquestions.com/interview/Behavioral/Tell-me-about-a-time-when-you-had-to-work-with-som-GQT168840.html

a situation where you took the lead to resolve conflict – not your manager or co-worker.[58]

You can google 'behavioural event interview questions and answers' to learn more about this type of interview question and read sample answers.

How to answer a BEI question when you don't have an example

If you are asked a BEI question about a situation you have not experienced, say that you haven't experienced that but offer to let them know what you would do in that situation.

If you are asked a BEI question and cannot think of a good example to give as an answer, say that you cannot think of an example and either ask to come back to it later in the interview or say what you would do in that situation.

Asking questions of the interviewers

At the end of the interview, you will be asked if you have any questions to ask the interviewers. Asking questions shows you are interested in the job and enables you to learn more about the company and the job.

Questions you might ask include:

- What are the key performance indicators for the role?

---

58 '35 behavioral interview questions to prepare for (with example answers)', *Indeed Career Guide*, 27 February 2021, https://www.indeed.com/career-advice/interviewing/most-common-behavioral-interview-questions-and-answers

- If you were to hire me, what might I expect in a typical day?[59]
- If I were the successful applicant, what would you expect from me in the first three months?
- How do employees develop and learn?
- What are the challenges of this position?[60]
- How do you evaluate performance?
- I know that there is a trend towards <xyz> in this industry. Is your company moving in this direction?
- Will I have an opportunity to meet those who would be part of my staff/my manager during the interview process?[61]
- Who would I be reporting to?[62]
- What would your ideal job applicant be like and how would they succeed in the role?[63]

---

59 R Gillett, A Cain and J Hadden, 'The best questions to ask at the end of every job interview', *Business Insider Australia*, 23 December 2016, https://www.businessinsider.com.au/questions-to-ask-at-end-of-job-interview-2016-4?r=US&IR=T
60 R Gillett, A Cain and J Hadden, 'The best questions to ask at the end of every job interview'
61 R Gillett, A Cain and J Hadden, 'The best questions to ask at the end of every job interview'
62 R Gillett, A Cain and J Hadden, 'The best questions to ask at the end of every job interview'
63 'Best questions to ask in an interview', *Hudson*, https://au.hudson.com/job-seekers/career-advice/job-interviews/best-questions-to-ask-in-an-interview

- Where do you see the company in three years and how would the person in this role contribute to this vision?[64] (This question is relevant to a senior job applicant.)
- What do you consider the biggest challenges in this role?[65]
- How would you describe the working culture here?[66]
- Do you have any concerns about my ability to do the role?[67]

How to end the interview

It is then time to close the interview. Express your interest in the position if you are still interested in it by this stage. Ask the interviewers about their timeline for deciding and when you can expect to hear back from them.[68]

Do not ask the employer to offer you the job at the end of the interview. They will probably refuse. The employer will likely have more interviewees to interview and, even if you are the last interviewed, the interviewers will need time to discuss amongst themselves before deciding who to employ.

When shaking the hand of each interviewer, thank them by name (which you will have memorised before the interview).

---

64 R Gillett, A Cain and J Hadden, 'The best questions to ask at the end of every job interview'
65 'Best questions to ask in an interview', *Hudson*
66 'Best questions to ask in an interview', *Hudson*
67 M Wilkinson, 'How to close an interview to ensure you leave a lasting impression, *Coburg Banks*, https://www.coburgbanks.co.uk/blog/candidate-tips/closing-an-interview/
68 R Gillett, A Cain and J Hadden, 'The best questions to ask at the end of every job interview'

As your interviewer guides you to the exit, be careful what you say. Don't let your guard down.

How to handle a second interview

Some companies invite successful interviewees from the first interview to attend a second interview before deciding who to offer the job to. How should you manage a second interview? The answer to this question depends on who is interviewing you at your second interview.

If it's the CEO or a senior manager, then it may be that you are the preferred interviewee and the purpose of the second interview is to meet senior staff to get their final approval to hire you. In this case, you will need to be able to talk with the interviewer about high-level company and industry directions and trends.

Alternatively, if technical people are interviewing you at your second interview then you need to prepare for technical questions.

If offered the job at your second interview, express your interest in it and ask for time to consider the offer and respond the next day to disconnect the offer from salary negotiation. See the chapter 'Salary negotiation'.

Video interviews

Ensure you're in a quiet, well-lit room. Test your webcam, microphone, speaker, and conferencing software before the interview to ensure it works.

Dress professionally. Don't wear a jacket and tie with your pyjama pants as the interviewers might be able to see your pyjama pants. Make sure that your drying clothes or messy room cannot be seen by the interviewers. Consider using a virtual background image.

Check that you are positioned in the middle of the screen the interviewers see. Ensure your face is illuminated from the front, preferably by natural light. Maintain eye contact with the interviewers by looking at the webcam instead of the screen.

Digital interviews

Digital interviews – in which you're given a set list of questions and record your answers on camera – are increasingly common in the hiring world, especially for first-round or screening interviews.

You'll have a minute or two to read and contemplate a question, then another couple minutes to answer it while a camera records you. Typically, a company will give you a time frame (something between two days and a week) to complete it on your own. During the interview, some organisations provide one redo if you mess up, others unlimited tries, depending on who it is.

Answering questions working against a clock can be tricky. If you find yourself ranting, don't be afraid to catch yourself and say, 'Sorry, I think I'm getting a bit off track. Here's what I mean to say...' They'll respect that you're self-aware and focused on the task at hand.

Prepare as you would for any face-to-face interview, but there are other things you can do to be prepared:

- Give yourself two minutes per response. If you go too long, consider cutting out the 'fat' or parts that don't directly answer the question.

- Practise your speech over your computer camera. You'll get comfortable with seeing your own face instead of an interviewer's.[69]

Apart from the above, what applies to video interviewing applies to digital interviews

Interviews while dining

Employers may take their leading job candidates out to lunch or dinner, especially when they are interviewing for jobs where there is a lot of client interaction, to evaluate their social skills and to see how the candidates handle themselves under pressure.

Don't order the most expensive item on the menu. Don't order something that is difficult to eat without making a mess.

Engage in a conversation. Dining interviews aren't one-sided. They are an opportunity for the interviewer to get to know you and vice versa.

If you drink alcohol, don't drink more than one glass. If you don't drink, politely decline if you're asked if you would like a drink.

---

69 A Kalish, 'How to nail your video assessment and actually get to meet the hiring manager in person', *The Muse*, https://www.themuse.com/advice/how-to-nail-your-video-assessment-and-actually-get-to-meet-the-hiring-manager-in-person

Don't offer to pay the bill.[70]

Companies employing graduates sometimes ask prospective employees to cocktail social functions. The above recommendations regarding alcohol apply here too. Be prepared to engage in small talk.

Group interviews

When an employer wants to meet multiple candidates at once, they may use a group interview. This is when you and other candidates are all interviewed at the same time. This type of interview can be challenging since you and your competition are right by each other, often answering the same questions.

How to stand out in a group interview

1. Don't try to blend in.

If you find that each candidate is answering a question in a similar way, try to find a way to add new insights when it's your turn to answer. Think about your own unique experiences and skill set when coming up with your answer. When the person before you has a genuinely good response, you could also build upon what they said to offer something new.

2. Show your leadership skills.

Volunteering to go first can show that you have the qualities of a leader. Even though group interviews can be intimidating,

---

[70] A Doyle, 'Tips for interviewing while dining', *The Balance Careers*, updated 26 August 2019, https://www.thebalancecareers.com/tips-for-interviewing-while-dining-2061318

they also give you the chance to prove how you can adapt to challenging situations.

3. Demonstrate your listening abilities.

It may be tempting to focus on your own responses, however it's more important to actively listen during your interview. By fully understanding what other candidates just said, you can come up with more meaningful answers. Make an effort to remember everyone's name and use names when referring to someone else's ideas. This can show the employer that you are both thoughtful and attentive to details.

Tips for succeeding in a group interview

- **Be friendly.** Even though you are competing for a job, be polite and professional to the other candidates.
- **Show confidence.** Speaking clearly, making eye contact, and sitting up straight are all ways to show that you are a confident person.
- **Be prepared.** Although you may not know which questions the employer may ask, it's still important to prepare for common interview questions.
- **Treat others with respect.** As another candidate is speaking, give them your undivided attention. Even if you have solid points to make, be sure to let everyone get a chance to speak.[71]

---

71 'How to stand out in a group interview', *Glassdoor*, https://www.glassdoor.com/blog/guide/group-interview/

Panel interviews

A panel interview is when you are interviewed by more than one interviewer.

Panel interviews involve a candidate answering questions from several different representatives of the business.

Treat all members of the panel equally. Look at each person when they speak to you and take time to introduce yourself to everyone.[72] When answering a question, look at each panellist, not just the one who asked you the question.

Bring enough materials for the entire panel.[73]

General interview tips

If you have been invited to an interview, the company is seriously considering you for the job. Employers don't waste their time interviewing people they think are unsuitable.

Don't exaggerate your level of experience as it is possible a referee check will uncover your exaggeration.

Switch your mobile phone to silent mode prior to the interview.

---

[72] Australian Government, 'Get your panel interview basics', *Job Jumpstart*, https://www.jobjumpstart.gov.au/article/get-your-panel-interview-basics

[73] 'How to succeed in a panel interview: tips and example questions', *Indeed Career Guide*, 30 November 2020, https://www.indeed.com/career-advice/interviewing/succeed-in-a-panel-interview

Managing nervousness

It's normal to be nervous at interviews. The best interviewers understand this and are good at relaxing interviewees to get the best out of them.

Manage your nerves by:

- preparing for your interview
- bringing notes you can refer to at the interview
- arriving early if the interview is face to face
- learning breathing techniques such as box breathing to help you relax
- visualising a successful interview
- realising there are other jobs if you miss out on this one
- realising feeling nervous is normal when you are being judged
- realising feeling nervous is normal when getting the job is important to you.

Reception area etiquette

If you sit in the reception area while waiting for your interview, you may find that when the interviewer greets you with a handshake you are still grasping your belongings and half-sitting, half-standing as you are getting up out of the chair. To prevent this less-than-favourable first impression:

- stand rather than sit in the reception area so you are ready to greet the interviewer face to face

- give the receptionist your bag or briefcase and coat to store so you don't have to carry them into the interview. Keep your notes and a pen with you.

What to do if you are running late

If you are running late for an interview, let the main interviewer know as soon as possible. Apologise and give the reason why you are running late. Let them know the time you expect to arrive. Accept that they may want to reschedule the interview. When you do get there, pause a moment before going inside to gain composure, especially if you are flustered due to rushing and/or being late. Apologise again at the start of the interview.

Should you accept the offer of a drink?

The danger of accepting is that you may spill the drink. If you hold a drink of water in your right hand while waiting in reception, then when the interviewer greets you with a handshake, they will feel the cold water on your hand due to the condensation.

If it's a warm day or you get hot while under pressure in the interview, then accepting water is wise. You might get a dry throat answering questions and need a glass of water.

How to know if you are giving the right answer to a question

When you're answering a question and you see the interviewers nodding their heads, you know that they like your answer, so finish your answer and wait for the next question. If they do not nod their heads, continue with your answer (within reason), saying other things you haven't yet mentioned, until they nod their heads.

Say what *you* did

Be careful answering a question saying, 'We did this …' If you did some tasks say, 'I did this …' If you were part of a team then say what part you played to assist the team.

How to answer a difficult question

If you are asked a difficult question, ask the interviewer to repeat the question. Sometimes they will word it differently or provide you with more information to help you answer. You can't do this for every question but for one or two questions you can.

Expect to be asked a question you haven't prepared an answer for.

What to do if you don't know the answer to a question

If you are asked a question you don't know the answer to:

- stay calm
- ask the interviewer to repeat/clarify the question
- don't make up an answer
- don't say 'I don't know'
- try to relate it to something you do know
- say you're not sure but will find out the answer after the interview
- email the answer to the interviewer.

How graduates can answer questions about their experience

Graduates may think they have no experience, however they have a lot of experience to draw on:

- Assignments
- Group work
- Practical work (experiments)
- Presentations
- Work experience
- Awards
- Volunteer roles in the community
- Club committee roles
- Hobbies
- Sport.

Illegal questions that employers and recruiters are not allowed to ask

- Ethnic/racial background
- Sexual orientation
- Age
- Religion
- Marital status
- Family plans (i.e. plans to have a baby)
- Voting habits

- Physical or mental disability status (unless it directly impacts the role)
- Union membership status.[74]

Some examples of how to respond to illegal questions include:

- Well, I don't know the answer to that question yet, however I'm very interested in the career paths your company can offer me. Do you mind telling me about them?
- It sounds like family and children are an important topic to you. I believe I have handled my childcare arrangements appropriately throughout my career in the industry.
- My age has never been a restricting barrier in any task I have accomplished throughout my career; I don't see how it would suddenly inhibit my job-related skill set.
- That question does not impact my ability to perform the required tasks. Would it be of value to you if I described my leadership skills in my previous roles instead?
- I'm confident that despite my family status, I can manage the dedication and future commitment that this position requires.

---

74 'Interviewing your candidate – you can't ask that!', *Employsure*, 21 June 2019, https://employsure.com.au/blog/illegal-interview-questions-not-to-ask-candidates/

- My religious practices are of great importance to me; however, I find they rarely interfere with my dedication to any position I undertake.[75]

If an employer asks if you have a back injury, which is an illegal question, you could reply that you can safely perform the duties of the job. If a small part of a job requires lifting, which you cannot do, say that you would need a lifting device or assistance to do that without disclosing you have a back injury.

Applying for a job when you have a criminal record

In some circumstances, there is a clear legal requirement that a job applicant should not have a certain criminal record. An employer may be obliged to ask a job applicant for criminal record details in these circumstances. Employers are, however, required to ask an employee to consent to a police check.

Even when there is no external obligation on an employer to enquire about a person's criminal record, employers may still ask a person if they have a criminal record. However, employers should only ask about a criminal record where there is a connection between the inherent requirements of a job and a criminal record.

Employers should only ask job applicants to disclose specific criminal record information if they have identified that certain criminal convictions or offences are relevant to the inherent requirements of the job.

---

75   S Caruso, '1 in 5 employers unknowingly ask illegal interview questions, Here's how to dodge them', *Training.com.au*, 27 July 2018, https://www.training.com.au/ed/1-in-5-employers-unknowingly-ask-illegal-interview-questions-heres-how-to-dodge-them/

If there is a requirement under legislation to disclose a criminal record, such as when working with children, then a job applicant must disclose their record. Otherwise, there is no absolute obligation for a job applicant to answer a question about their criminal record even when asked. However, if an employer asks a reasonable question – for example, a specific question about a criminal history relevant to the job – an employer may be entitled to refuse to hire a person based on failure to answer that reasonable question.

Some employers decide not to employ an applicant who has failed to disclose a criminal record, not because of the nature of the record, but because an inherent requirement of the job is honesty and trustworthiness, and the failure to make a disclosure is treated as dishonesty.

In most cases, there is no requirement to disclose a spent conviction. However, some kinds of employment, for example, employment where people will be working with children, are exempt from spent convictions legislation.

Criminal record checks should only be conducted with the written consent of the job applicant.

An employer will generally need to discuss the relevance of the criminal record with the job applicant or invite them to provide further information, in order to assess whether the person can meet the inherent requirements of the job.[76]

---

[76] 'Human Rights: On the record: recruitment (Chapter 5)', *Australian Human Rights Commission*, https://humanrights.gov.au/our-work/human-rights-record-recruitment-chapter-5

Use of humour in an interview

Don't make any jokes during the interview unless you have a good sense of humour and a suitable opportunity arises, in which case it can show that you would be a good person to work with. Err on the side of caution regarding humour. If the interview is formal and serious, don't use humour. If the interview is casual and friendly, and an opportunity arises, then you might use humour.

Should you send a thank you email after an interview?

Sending a thank you email after an interview is highly unlikely to make a difference to your chances of getting a job offer, but you can send one. If you did well in the interview but answered one question poorly, then sending an email that thanks the interviewers, reiterates your interest in the position, and gives the improved answer might be worth a try.

Face-to-face and video interviews key points

- Prepare for an interview by googling interview questions and answers to develop your answers to likely questions.

- Research the company and read the position description.

- Dress appropriately depending on the job you're applying for.

- Behavioural event interview questions are about past experiences because past behaviour is considered the best predictor of future behaviour. Answer these questions using the STAR (Situation – Task – Action – Result) framework.

- Prepare some questions for the interviewer to demonstrate your interest in the job and to find out more about the company and the job.

- For video interviews, ensure your technology works, dress professionally, and check your face is illuminated.

- When being interviewed with other candidates, don't try to blend in, listen carefully, and treat others with respect.

- When answering a question of a panel member, look at each panelist.

- When preparing for digital interviews where you're given a list of questions and record your responses on camera, limit the length of your answers and become used to looking at your face on the screen by practising your answers.

Interview feedback

If you're invited to an interview but don't get the job, should you request feedback? Yes. Finding out what your interviewers thought of your interview performance may improve your performance at your next interview.

If they phone to let you know you were unsuccessful, ask for feedback. If you're not available and they leave you a phone message, phone them back to request feedback. If they don't answer their phone, leave a message for them to call you back. Don't leave the interviewer a phone message asking for interview feedback as they are less likely to return your call.

If they let you know you were unsuccessful by email, phone them back as your chance of getting meaningful feedback is higher than having them respond to an email.

When speaking with an interviewer, thank them again for the interview and say that you are open to honest feedback to improve your future interview performance. Don't ask why you weren't hired. Some interviewers will not provide honest feedback. Rather than saying that you handled several questions poorly, they may say other interviewees had more experience or give you another possibly false reason. Sometimes an interviewer will not give interview feedback.

If an interviewer does give feedback, accept what they say. Don't argue with them or become defensive. Thank them for their feedback. They might say that you performed well at the interview despite not being offered the job and that they would be happy to receive an application from you if another vacancy occurs. If so, ask if it's okay to keep in touch with them. If they agree, ask if it's okay to phone/email them and ask how often you should contact them.

Interview feedback key points

- Upon hearing that you have missed out on a job, ask for feedback to improve your future interview performance.

- Accept feedback without becoming defensive or disagreeing with the interviewer.

- Some interviewers will not provide genuine feedback by saying other applicants performed better.

Assessment centres

An assessment centre tests your abilities in a group setting so assessors can predict your performance in the workplace. The term 'assessment centre' does not refer to a physical place, but rather a series of recruitment activities.

What happens at an assessment centre

You're invited to a location or online (virtual assessment centre) for a half or full day with groups of candidates to participate in a series of exercises, some of which will simulate those encountered in the real workplace. Assessment centres are used primarily by medium and large organisations – including those with internship and graduate programs – and the location can be the organisation's office, a recruitment agency, or a hotel conference facility.

Trained assessors assess your behaviour and performance against a set of pre-established criteria. Based on your individual performance, an organisation predicts how well you would perform in the workplace and fit with the organisational culture.

What you need to do at an assessment centre

Typical tasks are:

- group exercises like problem-solving, strategising, or debating tasks
- verbal presentations to test your ability to structure a presentation and clearly communicate information to others
- role plays where you need to act out a work-related situation
- in-tray exercises where you are given a full 'in-tray' of memos, emails, and phone messages typical of the role or level you're seeking, and are asked to prioritise each task and act on items within a time limit.[77]

What you must do to perform to the best of your ability in group assessment exercises:

- Be yourself at all times. Don't try to project a different image that you will not be able to sustain and will be detrimental in the long run.
- Don't talk just for the sake of talking. The quality of what you say is likely to be more important than the quantity.
- Listen carefully to what other members of the group say but don't lapse into silence.

---

[77] The University of Sydney, Careers Centre, 'Assessment centres', *The University of Sydney*, https://www.sydney.edu.au/careers/students/applying-for-jobs/assessment-centres.html

- Try to make as many positive contributions to the discussion as circumstances permit. By keeping quiet you are missing an opportunity to demonstrate your strengths.
- People with very different styles can perform with equal effectiveness – it is not a competition to see who can dominate the interactions of the group.

What assessors are looking for:

- Are you able to help the group achieve the objectives?
- Can you think on your feet?
- Can you speak effectively in front of others by expressing your views clearly and making yourself heard by the rest of the group?
- Can you inject some structure into the discussion, e.g. by helping the group to organise its ideas to frame a coherent response?
- Can you build on what others say, e.g. in order to broaden the discussion or the collective analysis of the problem?
- Can you help to get the best out of the group, e.g. by drawing others into the discussion or by challenging those who are wasting the group's time on irrelevancies?
- Can you help to drive the group forward, e.g. by suggesting ways of completing the task at hand?

The assessors will be looking for competence or ability to develop competence in the following areas:

- interpersonal skills including your ability to empathise with others
- leadership skills including your ability to influence others
- communication skills – both verbal and non-verbal
- focus on results including goal orientation, motivation, and achievement drive
- working with others including your teamwork skills.[78]

Job applicants can be individually interviewed and/or undergo psychometric testing on the same day as the assessment centre.

---

78 H Tolley and R Wood 2011, *How to succeed at an assessment centre: essential preparation for psychometric tests, group and role-play exercises, panel interviews and presentations*, Kogan Page, London

Assessment centres key points

- An assessment centre tests your abilities in a group setting so assessors can predict your performance in the workplace.
- You're invited to a location or online for a half or full day with groups of candidates to participate in a series of exercises.
- Trained assessors assess your behaviour and performance.
- Typical tasks are group exercises like problem-solving, strategising, or debating tasks.
- To perform to the best of your ability in group assessment exercises be yourself at all times, don't talk just for the sake of talking, listen carefully and try to make many positive contributions to the discussion.[79]

---

[79] The University of Sydney, Careers Centre, 'Typical tasks are group exercises like problem-solving, strategising, or debating tasks', *The University of Sydney*, https://www.sydney.edu.au/careers/students/applying-for-jobs/assessment-centres.html

Psychometric testing

Some companies use psychometric tests to screen job applicants. They measure the ability to perform well in a job. They are used because there is a strong correlation between test scores and job performance.[80] These tests are often used in graduate recruitment which is highly competitive. There are different types of psychometric tests. The most common tests in recruitment are:[81]

- verbal reasoning
- numerical reasoning
- personality
- logical reasoning
- situational judgement.

If you know a company is going to ask you to complete one or more tests, you can ask what type(s) they are going to use. You can google 'practice psychometric tests' to become familiar and more comfortable with the types of questions. Trying to change the result of a test by practising may get you a job that you cannot or don't want to do.

---

80 'Our complete guide to psychometric tests', *Assessment Day*, https://www.assessmentday.co.uk/psychometric-test.htm
81 'The top five psychometric tests used in recruitment', *INDVSTRVS*, https://indvstrvs.com/psychometric-tests/

Tips for taking psychometric tests

Make sure you are well rested and won't be interrupted. Read the instructions carefully. Take a break between tests if you can.

If you're unsuccessful, try not to be too concerned and stay positive.

Salary negotiation

This chapter details how to negotiate a higher salary than what you are offered.

Don't ask about salary before or during your interview. If asked about your salary expectations early in the interview, say that you don't yet know enough about the job. If the interviewer persists in asking you, then politely ask if you are being offered the job. Alternatively, you can say, 'I am open to a fair and reasonable offer.' Never state a figure, because if you state a low figure, the employer may agree and then you're working for less than you could have achieved. If you state a high figure, the employer may not want to hire you, thinking you may leave for a higher paid job or won't accept their job offer.

Often an employer will ask your current or most recent salary because they are wanting to pay you a little more to keep you happy if it's less than or equal to what they have budgeted. Your current or previous job duties may be different to the job you are applying for and therefore a comparison of salaries may be invalid. Politely refuse to state your current or recent salary due to confidentiality even if you are not bound by confidentiality. Don't lie by saying you earn a higher salary than you earn.

Many entry-level positions have a fixed hourly rate and there is no opportunity to negotiate salary. If salary is negotiable, wait until you're offered the job before starting to negotiate. This is because early on when all the interviewees are being interviewed, you don't have much negotiating power. When you're offered the job, the company has been through a potentially lengthy selection process to make their hiring decision and needs to get you started as soon as possible. If an employee has left the job, the company will want a replacement person to commence as soon as possible. If the position is new, the company will have identified a need for a person to do the work and will want to hire someone promptly. The fact they need to have a person start as soon as possible and have made you a job offer means you have negotiating power for salary and conditions as they won't want to lose you for a small amount of money and then have to find someone else. In the experience of the author, they will offer you about 5% less than what you can negotiate. They want to employ you at the lowest figure in the salary band for your job level.

When they phone and offer you the job for a stated salary, say that you are very interested and will let them know that afternoon or first thing the next morning. The reason for this is to separate the offer from the salary negotiation.

When you call them back, reiterate your interest in the position and state your case for a higher salary. You might say that your research has found two other competitor companies are paying $X and $Y respectively and ask if they could review the proposed salary in the light of that information. Or you could ask them to review the salary given your level of qualifications and experience. They might ask you what salary you are wanting. Respond by saying that you don't have a figure in mind as they might offer you a higher figure. HR won't have the authority to increase the salary offer and will have to speak with the hiring manager who will decide if they will increase their offer. If they call you back with an offer of an increased salary, you can decide if you want to accept it. Don't try for a further increase as you would be unlikely to get much, if anything, and you risk damaging your relationship with your new employer.

If you have another job offer, you can play one employer off against the other. Don't tell each company the name of the other company. You could say you have another offer of $X and ask your preferred company to match it. Each company will realise that you are a sought-after employee. Only do this when you have another offer.

If they cannot increase your salary, then you need to decide if you want to accept or politely decline the offer. To accept, you could say that you are so interested in the role that you would like to accept.

If a company cannot increase the salary, then other benefits may be able to be negotiated, such as a mobile phone or use of a work car for personal use, however for many jobs, these things are non-negotiable.

Asking about salary before applying or being interviewed

It's a lot of work writing a job application and preparing for an interview, only to find at the end of the process that the salary offer is way too low. You can try asking for the salary range before applying. For example: 'I want to be respectful of your company's time. Would you please tell me the salary band for the job?'

Not applying for jobs with low salaries

Some people don't apply for a job because the salary is low but still above any relevant award. However, it may be better to apply and start the job if you don't get any other offers. You can always stay in the job while you look for a better paying job or stay there for six months which is long enough to include it in your resume.

Salary negotiation key points

- Don't negotiate before receiving a job offer.
- Don't disclose your current or most recent salary.
- Don't say how much you want.
- After receiving a job offer, ask the employer if they can review the proposed salary given your qualifications and experience.

Handling multiple job offers

What if you get a job offer from company <one> while you are waiting for another job offer from company <two> where you would prefer to work?

The best approach is to:

1. thank company <one> for the job offer
2. say you are very interested
3. ask when you should expect to receive the offer in writing.

Then phone company <two> to explain that you are under offer and ask where their selection process is at. You may need to accept the first job offer and await the hiring decision of company <two>. If a job offer is made by company <two> and after some negotiation you accept, then you can contact company <one> to say that you will not be accepting their offer.

You don't want to reject the first job offer as you may not receive any other offers. Hence, a cautious approach to protect your interests is to accept the first job offer even if you are confident of further offers. Accepting the first company's offer and later declining the job won't make you popular with that company but at least you will be working in your preferred job.

Overqualified job seeker

It is difficult to secure a job for which you are overqualified.

The reasons employers are reluctant to hire overqualified job seekers are that they:

- think you will continue to job search to find a more senior job
- think you will become bored with lower level work
- think you will be unhappy with lower pay and will look for higher paid work
- will be concerned whether you will be able to take direction.

How to tailor your resume to appear less overqualified

- Include the job title in your Career Summary.
- Explain in your Career Summary why you are applying for a lower level job.
- Leave out higher degrees.
- Include lower level duties you did and leave out higher level duties.

- Remove a higher level job if it does not create too much of a gap.

- Consider a functional resume (refer to the 'Resume format' section in the 'Resume writing' chapter).

Explain why you are the right person for the job in your cover letter. Perhaps you are close to retirement, coming out of retirement, returning from maternity leave, or want a better work-life balance.

Underqualified job seeker

Don't apply for jobs you are obviously underqualified for. Apply for jobs where you meet 80% of the requirements. For example, if:

- you have one years' experience and they ask for three to five years, they may be willing to consider your application if your experience is relevant.
- they ask for a master's degree and you have a bachelor's degree, it may still be worthwhile applying.[82]

If you're unsure whether to apply for a job, err on the side of applying. However, if an employer states that a certain qualification or experience is essential and you don't have it, there is little point in applying even if you meet the other requirements.

If you're an assistant accountant applying for accountant jobs and some accountants apply, you're not likely to be interviewed unless you have been performing many of the tasks accountants perform and you have the same qualifications as the accountants. Another pathway for an assistant accountant to become an accountant may be through internal promotion. Browsing LinkedIn profiles of accountants who were assistant accountants at the same company will identify companies that

---

82 N Autenrieth, 'How to be a great candidate even if you're under-qualified for the job', *TopResume©*, https://au.topresume.com/career-advice/be-a-great-candidate-even-if-youre-under-qualified-for-the-job

promote assistant accountants. Assistant accountants wanting to become accountants could target assistant accountant jobs at those companies. Each company would need to have many accountants working there, not just one accountant.

Accountant roles that don't require a large amount of experience and are offering entry level salary may deter experienced accountants from applying, enabling an assistant accountant to be competitive in the recruitment process.

If you're submitting good quality, well-written job applications and you are consistently not getting any interviews, it's likely that your job applications are not competitive for those jobs. After checking with a career counsellor, HR professional or recruiter friend that your applications are of good quality, an option may be to access the hidden job market. See the chapter 'Accessing the hidden job market'.

Graduates can reasonably apply for jobs that require one years' experience, however their job application would need to be well written and include their university experience and any internship and work experience.

Mature age job seekers

Mature age job seekers are defined as being aged 45+. Discrimination against mature age job seekers in the labour market has been documented in government reports.[83]

The author's experience in assisting mature age people to find work is that many of these people are too focused on age discrimination. Accept that it occurs and can be addressed by the following measures:

- Include only the last ten years or so of employment in your resume.
- Remove any education dates in your resume unless gained recently.
- Delete the year or the age from your email address. For example, fred1952@hotmail.com or fred64@hotmail.com might enable an employer to deduce a person's age.

If you are concerned about age-based discrimination don't add a photo to your LinkedIn profile.

---

83 CEPAR, ARC Centre of Excellence in Population Ageing Research 2019, *Maximising potential: findings from the Mature Workers in Organisations Survey (MWOS)*, p.5, CEPAR, https://cepar.edu.au/sites/default/files/Findings-from-Mature-Workers-in-Organisations-Survey-Dec-2019.pdf

While it's possible for an employer to discriminate based on age at an interview, the interviewee has an opportunity to meet the employer and do well at the interview and change the mindset of the employer.

Is it easier to find work when you're working?

A study[84] found that employed people were more likely to receive unsolicited contact from a potential employer or a referral from a contact than unemployed people. Their response rate from employers was four times that of unemployed applicants. They got more than twice the interviews and three times as many offers per application.[85]

Advantages of job seeking when you're working:

- No recent gaps in your resume.
- You don't have to explain why you're not working.
- You don't have to accept the first job offer you get because of your finances.

Disadvantages of job seeking when you're working:

---

84   RJ Faberman, Al Mueller, A Şahin & G Topa, *Job search behavior among the employed and non-employed*, National bureau of Economic Research, https://www.nber.org/system/files/working_papers/w23731/w23731.pdf

85   C Purtill, 'The biggest mistake people make when searching for a job is not acting like they already have one', *Quartz*, 12 April 2017, https://qz.com/955079/research-proves-its-easier-to-get-a-job-when-you-already-have-a-job/

- You have to be secretive in your job search so your employer doesn't find out.
- You have less time to search because you're working.

Advantages of job seeking when you're unemployed:

- You have more time to job search.
- You don't have to be secretive in your job search.

Disadvantages of job seeking when you're unemployed:

- You may be more desperate to accept the first job offer than someone who is working.
- You don't get invited to interviews due to gaps in your resume.

The dos and don'ts of job searching while you're employed

Dos

- Make sure your LinkedIn profile is 100% complete.
- Schedule interviews during non-work hours.
- Stay focused on your current job.

Don'ts

- Don't tell anyone at work.
- Never bad-mouth your current employer.
- Don't use any of your current co-workers or supervisors as referees.
- Don't use the company computer, internet, fax machine, [email] or phone in your job search.
- Don't dress differently than normal. Bring your interview clothes with you to work and change in the car or the restroom when you get to your destination.

- Don't mention your job search on social media.
- Don't post your resume on job boards.[86]

---

[86] J Smith, 'The dos and don'ts of job searching while you're still employed', *Forbes*, 26 October 2012, https://www.forbes.com/sites/jacquelynsmith/2012/10/26/the-dos-and-donts-of-job-searching-while-youre-still-employed/?sh=4ca349ba7e07

Finding work in the gig economy

A gig economy is a free market system in which temporary positions are common and organisations hire independent workers for short-term commitments. The term 'gig' is a slang word for a job that lasts a specified period of time; it is typically used by musicians.[87]

It is beyond the scope of this book to discuss the pros and cons of the gig economy or the skill set required to be successful.

Google 'gig economy websites' and 'gig economy apps' to find ads for this type of work.

---

[87] AS Gillis, 'Gig economy', *WhatIs.com®*, https://whatis.techtarget.com/definition/gig-economy

Finding work for people with a disability

Job seeking for people with a disability is the same as for the general population, however some additional factors need to be considered:

- Whether to disclose your disability.
- Workplace modifications.
- Supported wage system.
- Customised employment.
- Supported employment.

Consider whether to disclose your disability

The disability disclosure chart in Appendix J lists the advantages and disadvantages of disclosing a disability at each stage of the job application process.

If a disability does not affect your work performance and you don't need to take many days off work, then there is no need to disclose your disability to an employer.

How to disclose your disability at an interview

If you choose to disclose a disability, make it brief and positive near the start of the interview. For example, you could say, 'I have a hearing disability and manage by lip reading, using email and TTY.'[88]

Workplace modifications

A person starting or already working in a job may be eligible for workplace modifications paid for by the government. When a person leaves a job, they may take the modification, e.g. a special chair, with them.

Supported wage system (SWS)

The SWS is for employees with a disability who are unable to perform jobs at the same productivity level as other employees. It allows employers to pay wages based on the workplace productivity of a person with a disability, however the formal workplace agreement must include arrangements for SWS if they want to apply for SWS. If an employer makes an application for SWS, their employee with a disability will need to have an SWS assessment from a qualified assessor.

The assessment will:

- be done with the employer, the employee with a disability, and the Disability Employment Services provider and nominee (if the employee has one) at a time that suits everyone

---

88 A TTY is a special device that lets people who are deaf, hard of hearing, or speech-impaired use the telephone to communicate.

- happen on an employee's regular workday when they are doing their usual job.

The assessor will look at information such as the employee's job description, time spent on each duty, hours and days worked, break times, and the level of supervision required.

The assessor will also make sure that any modifications that the employee needs to do their job are in place.[89]

Customised employment (CE)

CE is a way of personalising the employment relationship between a candidate and an employer in order to meet the needs of both. It applies in particular to employees with disabilities. The individual employee's skills, interests and needs are identified in a process of 'discovery', and job content and environment are tailored to these in a process of negotiation.[90]

CE may include assisting a person with a disability to start and run a small business.

It is outside of the scope of this book to go into further detail, however googling 'customised employment' (and the US spelling 'customized employment') may be a first step to accessing a provider of this assistance.

---

89 Australian Government, 'Supported Wage System (SWS)', *Job Access*, updated 29 June 2021, https://www.jobaccess.gov.au/supported-wage-system-sws

90 Wikipedia, 'Customized employment', *Wikipedia, the Free Encyclopedia*, updated 20 October 2020, https://en.wikipedia.org/wiki/Customized_employment

Supported employment

Supported employment is when businesses employ mostly people with a disability and support them in their job. Supported employees are usually people who work in Australian Disability Enterprises (ADEs) that provide work as varied as packaging, assembly, production, recycling, screen-printing, plant nursery, garden maintenance and landscaping, cleaning services, laundry services and food services.[91]

The majority of supported employees working in ADEs are employed under the Supported Employment Services Award 2020. This award, for supported employees, is calculated using a number of wage assessment tools. These tools decide what proportion of wage the employee will be paid. Under this system, ADE employees can get paid as little as $2.37 an hour.[92]

---

91 Australian Government, 'Supported employment' section in 'Australian Government support at work', *Job Access*, updated 8 March 2019, https://www.jobaccess.gov.au/people-with-disability/australian-government-support-work

92 E Wright and Team's C Edmonds, 'Royal commission hears Australian disability enterprise workers paid as little as $2.50 an hour', 13 April 2022, https://www.abc.net.au/news/2022-04-13/disability-royal-commission-probes-ade-employment-jobs-wages/100977448

Finding work for people with a disability key points

- Job seeking for people with a disability is the same as for the general population, however some additional factors need to be considered.

- There are advantages and disadvantages of disclosing a disability at each stage of the job application process.

- A person starting or already working in a job may be eligible for workplace modifications paid for by the government.

- The supported wage system is for employees with a disability who are unable to perform jobs at the same productivity level as other employees.

- In customised employment the individual employee's skills, interests and needs are identified in a process of 'discovery', and job content and environment are tailored to these in a process of negotiation.

- Supported employment is when businesses employ mostly people with a disability and support them in their job.

Applying for work in another state

An employer is more likely to hire job seekers who live locally. Not all job seekers applying for work in another state will commit to relocating. Delete your current address from your resume and cover letter.

If contacted by an employer or recruiter for an interview, explain why you are applying for a job in another state.

More credible answers include relocating because:

- your partner has found work in the other state
- your family live in the other state
- after spending time in the other state, you would like to move there.

Graduate student employment

Many students start thinking about getting a job after finishing their final exam. However, students need to start building their employability from the start of their course by doing:

- volunteer roles
- paid part-time/casual work
- extra-curricular activities.

Students can access information about careers through their educator's website to enable them to write a resume, cover letter, develop interview skills, respond to selection criteria and apply for part-time/casual work. Students can book a session with a career counsellor for individual career guidance to learn how to enhance their employability. Careers centres will provide feedback on a student's resume and cover letter. Attending careers workshops will assist a student to understand what they need to do to enhance their employability once they finish their study. Generally, alumni may access their educator's careers centre for job search assistance by a career counsellor if they finished their last exam less than a year ago.

Taking on a committee and/or leadership role in an extra-curricular activity will grow a student's employability skills while adding to their resume. Performing course-related work experience in the vacation prior to the final year can result in an offer of full-time work upon course completion. Joining a relevant professional association as a student member can result in growing a student's knowledge of and network of contacts in their field.

Many companies seeking graduates start advertising at the start of the final year of study. Annual careers fairs held early in the year provide an opportunity for students to talk with company representatives. Competition for top tier company graduate program jobs is very strong. For this reason, some final year students may find more success in focusing their applications at mid-tier companies who perhaps don't attend the careers fairs.

Further information to assist graduates is provided in the chapters 'Resume writing', 'Referees', 'Assessment centres', 'Underqualified job seeker', and the section 'How graduates can answer questions about their experience' in the chapter 'Face-to-face and video interviews'.

Professional year programs

A professional year program is a structured professional development program combining formal learning and workplace experience for international students who have graduated from a university in Australia.[92]

Local experience can also be gained from unpaid internships/ professional year courses, however:

- the Fair Work Ombudsman is of the view that work should be paid. Unpaid trials may be legal but should range from one hour to one shift.*
- some companies take unfair advantage of job seekers by having them work for no pay with no opportunity of becoming a paid employee.
- be alert to scam companies offering unpaid internships/ professional year courses.
- the terms of the internship need to be clarified before starting.

* See note on following page.

---

92 'The benefits of an Australian Professional Year Program', *Studies in Australia*, https://www.studiesinaustralia.com/Blog/life-after-study/the-benefits-of-an-australian-professional-year-program

NOTE: Sometimes an employer might ask a person to do an unpaid trial while they evaluate them for a vacant job. This is used to determine if the person is suitable for the job by getting them to demonstrate their skills and is sometimes called a work trial. Unpaid work trials may be unlawful where:

- it isn't necessary to demonstrate the skills required for the job or has continued for longer than is actually needed. This will be dependent on the nature and complexity of the work but could range from an hour to one shift
- it involves more than only a demonstration of the person's skills, where they are directly relevant to a vacant position, or
- the person is not under direct supervision for the trial.

Any period beyond what is reasonably required to demonstrate the skills required for the job must be paid at the appropriate minimum rate of pay. If an employer wants to further assess a candidate's suitability, they could employ the person as a casual employee and/or for a probationary period and pay them accordingly for all hours worked.[93]

---

93 Australian Government, Fair Work Ombudsman, 'Unpaid trials', *Fair Work Ombudsman*, https://www.fairwork.gov.au/pay/unpaid-work/unpaid-trials

Immigrants

This chapter covers issues immigrants may have when seeking work.

Applying for work before arriving in your new country

Getting a job in your new country before migrating is difficult unless you have experience that is in high demand.

Including your current address when applying for jobs in your new country is likely to be unsuccessful due to the number of suitable local applicants. Hence it's best to exclude your current address. Including an overseas phone number is also likely to be the cause of an unsuccessful job application. You might use the phone number/address of a relative or friend who is in the new country, however if invited to an interview, you will need to explain that you are relocating and hope the employer will still consider your application.

Job seeking after immigration

Recognition of overseas qualifications

Immigrants may be able to get their overseas qualifications recognised by a government body. Google 'recognition of overseas qualifications' to find out how this works. Depending on your qualification and local regulations, you may need to get it recognised or sit an exam prior to starting work. Your qualification may not be recognised in your new country.

Language

If you are relocating to an English-speaking country and your first language is not English, get your resume, cover letters, and selection criteria responses reviewed by someone who has good English skills. Many job applications from immigrants contain poor grammar and poorly worded sentences.

If your first language is not English, improve your spoken and written English skills to help with your job search. Perform volunteer roles to improve your spoken and written English and to become accustomed to local workplace culture. If many people are having difficulty understanding your English, consider getting professional training from an English pronunciation specialist to become more understandable.

Networking

When looking for work, use LinkedIn to network with people from your previous country who are working in your occupation in your new country. Refer to the chapters 'Accessing the hidden job market' and 'LinkedIn as a job search tool' to find out how to network using LinkedIn.

As aforementioned in the 'Resume writing' chapter, studies show that people with foreign names are less likely to be invited to an interview than those with Anglo-sounding names. If you are concerned about this form of discrimination, you may consider anglicising your name in your resume.[94]

Lack of local experience

Often, feedback from an unsuccessful interview is that the job seeker lacks local experience, but this can be deduced by the employer prior to the interview by browsing a resume. Hence the job seeker should discount this feedback as an excuse when an interviewer does not want to give the real reason for missing out on the job.

Note that there are two components to experience: technical skills and employability skills. Employability skills include communication, teamwork, problem solving, initiative, planning/organising, learning, technology, and self-management. Generally, technical skills are the same the world over. As aforementioned, you can gain experience in local workplace culture through volunteer roles.

Difficulty finding work

If you're having difficulty finding work, consider applying for work that is one level below the job level you last worked in your home country as it may make work easier to find.

Having to change occupation

Some immigrants are unable to work in the occupation they had qualified for/worked in in their country of origin because:

---

[94] A Booth, 'Job hunt success is all in a name', *The Sydney Morning Herald*, 4 March 2013, https://www.smh.com.au/opinion/job-hunt-success-is-all-in-a-name-20130303-2feci.html

- their qualification is not recognised in their new country
- the job does not exist in the new country
- they gained a qualification in their country of origin but never gained any experience in that field
- the level of English required is higher than the immigrant currently has.

This results in the immigrant choosing and applying for different work to what they have done. For example, it is common for a person to apply for administration assistant jobs despite never having worked in this occupation. Without a qualification or experience in this new work field, the chance of obtaining employment is nil. The best option is to gain a certificate level qualification and do some relevant voluntary work to increase the chance of finding a job. Highlighting any administrative duties in previous jobs in your resume, cover letter, and selection criteria responses will help demonstrate you have some relevant experience.

Changing your resume to avoid possible discrimination

To avoid possible discrimination, delete any foreign university/college names from your resume unless the qualification was gained in the USA or the UK. Delete overseas countries and cities from the Employment History section of your resume. Delete the language section from your resume unless the job ad specifically requires a language other than English. If your duties or accomplishment statements contain a currency amount, convert it to the local currency of your new country. Don't include your work rights in your resume. If your right to work is limited, mention it briefly and positively at an interview.

Job applications and work culture differences between countries

Find out how job applications, accessing the hidden job market, and work culture differ between your country of origin and your new country. For example, in Colombia in Latin America, it is normal for a job seeker to be asked personal questions in an interview. As a result, it's common for these job seekers to include personal information in their job applications. In other countries, it is illegal and potentially discriminatory for employers to ask about an applicant's personal information.

Another cultural issue is where Chinese job seekers frame job applications as an opportunity for obtaining training and experience from the employer. However, in Australia, employers are interested in the skills and experience the employee will bring to the company.

In some countries, reference letters written by a former employer about the job seeker are attached to a job application. In Australia, listing the names and contact details of referees who can be contacted by phone is standard practice.

Overseas referees

Ideally, an immigrant will have at least one local referee. If referees are located overseas, then upon request from an employer, supply referee contact details together with the best hours in the new country's time zone to contact them.

Immigrants key points

- Getting a job in your new country before migrating is difficult unless you have experience that is in high demand.

- Immigrants may be able to get their overseas qualifications recognised by a government body.

- If you are relocating to an English-speaking country and your first language is not English, get your resume, cover letters, and selection criteria responses reviewed by someone who has good English skills.

- When looking for work, use LinkedIn to network with people from your previous country who are working in your occupation in your new country.

- If you're having difficulty finding work, consider applying for work that is one level below the job level you last worked in your home country as it may make work easier to find.

- To avoid possible discrimination, delete any foreign university/college names from your resume unless the qualification was gained in the USA or the UK.

- Find out how job applications, accessing the hidden job market, and work culture differ between your country of origin and your new country.

Long-term unemployment

Long-term unemployment is defined as being without paid work, and/or have been looking for work, for a year or more.[95]

How to get a job after long-term unemployment

1. Develop your skills

Use your time while looking for a job to earn skills and experience to benefit your career. Consider the abilities required of the jobs you'd like to have and take steps to develop them.

2. Education

Learning more about your field and receiving formal training can be an integral part of developing as a job candidate. Independently studying the requirements of your desired job at your local library can save financial resources. You could also take [low-fee/no upfront fee/no fee] classes ... that relate to the position you want.

---

[95] N Cassidy et al., 'Long-term unemployment in Australia', *Reserve Bank of Australia*, 10 December 2020, https://www.rba.gov.au/publications/bulletin/2020/dec/long-term-unemployment-in-australia.html

Professional certifications can also boost your visibility in the job market.[96]

Training courses can be a great way to build your skills and add new qualifications to your resume. If you've been out of work for a while you may feel a bit intimidated going straight into employment. A training course can help ease you in while teaching you valuable new skills that you can take forward into a new job role.[97]

3. Re-examine employment strategies and tactics[98]

Consider making some changes to your job searching strategy by reading this book in full, especially the chapters 'Accessing the hidden job market' and 'Job search strategy'.

4. Gaps in your resume

If you're concerned about a gap in the Employment History section of your resume, you can structure it in a way that highlights the quality of your experiences rather than the timeframes of your formal employment. The functional resume format (see the 'Resume format' section in the 'Resume writing' chapter and 'Appendix A: Functional resume template') highlights key experiences and skills rather than your chronological history of work. Using this resume style can demonstrate to employers that

---

96 'How to find a job after long-term unemployment', *Indeed Career Guide*, 1 March 2021, https://www.indeed.com/career-advice/finding-a-job/how-to-find-a-job-after-long-term-unemployment
97 'How to get back into work after long term unemployment?', *Building Better Opportunities*, https://bbostaffs.org/knowledge-advice/going-back-to-work-after-unemployment/
98 L Buhl, 'Breaking out of long-term unemployment', *Monster*, https://www.monster.com/career-advice/article/breaking-out-of-longterm-unemployment-hot-jobs

you are qualified for a job even if you have a long gap between positions.[99]

An alternate strategy to fill the gap is to do something you can fill the gap with. For example, if you're a programmer, write some code to perform a particular function. If you're a shoe designer, design yourself some shoes.[100] Starting a very small business can fill the gap.

5. Networking

If you've been out of circulation for a while, you have to remind people you're still around. You're also likely to be a little rusty in networking, so it's important to get out once or twice a week at least for a face-to-face meeting, lunch or networking event.[101] See the 'Networking with people' section in the chapter 'Accessing the hidden job market'.

6. Try volunteering

Lack of recent experience can be a big stumbling block for people who have been out of work for a long period. But there are ways around it. If you find this is the case for you, why not give volunteer roles a try? Not only can a volunteer role help to build your skills, give you a recent referee, and contribute to your experience, it can also help build your confidence and get you back into a 'working' mindset. See the 'Volunteering' chapter for further information.

Temporary roles and work placements can also help you to boost your confidence and get more work experience. Not only that

---

99 'How to find a job after long-term unemployment', *Indeed Career Guide*
100 L Buhl, 'Breaking out of long-term unemployment', *Monster*
101 L Buhl, 'Breaking out of long-term unemployment', *Monster*

but being proactive in this way shows that you are committed to finding employment and allows you to demonstrate your skills and capability to an employer.[102]

Tips for finding a job after long-term unemployment

- **Stay active**

Keeping up an exercise schedule can add structure to your day, which is important when you rejoin the workforce.[103] Being active helps you to relax, keeps you feeling strong, and is a healthy way to fill up your day.[104]

- **Set and keep a routine**

Without a job to structure your days, it's natural to feel a bit directionless. Set up an easy morning routine you can commit to on the weekdays. While waking up early, making breakfast, and checking jobs for an hour may seem minor, it gives your day purpose. They are small victories but victories nonetheless. Keeping busy and feeling productive will help you to relax and focus.

Stay social by setting up regular evening plans with your friends each week. It will not only give you something to look forward to

---

102 'How to get back into work after long term unemployment?', *Building Better Opportunities*
103 'How to find a job after long-term unemployment', *Indeed Career Guide*
104 L Pham, 'Here's what long-term unemployment looks like', *Career Contessa*, https://www.careercontessa.com/advice/long-term-unemployment/

but it could also be a way to subtly network and learn about new opportunities.[105]

- **Seek help**

Your friends can be a great resource in helping you find a job. Consider asking one of them to be an accountability partner to ensure you're meeting your application goals. For example, you could check in with your accountability partner on Fridays to let them know you've applied for a set number of jobs. You could also ask your friend to conduct mock interviews with you so you can practise answers to common interview questions.

Being unemployed long-term can be challenging, but you can seek professional help to keep up a positive attitude. Career counsellors and mental health professionals are both available to encourage you to meet your employment goals.[106]

- **Consider not using the term 'unemployed'**

When someone asks what you're doing now, don't say you're out of work. Talk about the projects you've done and what you're learning, and then mention, 'I'm looking for a paid position like this.'[107]

---

105 L Pham, 'Here's what long-term unemployment looks like', *Career Contessa*
106 'How to find a job after long-term unemployment', *Indeed Career Guide*
107 L Buhl, 'Breaking out of long-term unemployment', *Monster*

Long-term unemployment key points

- Long-term unemployment is defined as being without paid work, and/or have been looking for work, for a year or more.[108]

- Use your time while looking for a job to earn qualifications, skills, and experience to benefit your career.

- Consider making some changes to your job searching strategy by reading this book in full, especially the chapters 'Accessing the hidden job market' and 'Job search strategy'.

- Try volunteering in an area where you'll learn skills relevant to your job search.

- Try networking by meeting people who may be able to assist you in your job search.

- Set and keep to a routine.

- Seek help when you need.

---

108 N Cassidy et al., 'Long-term unemployment in Australia', *Reserve Bank of Australia*, 10 December 2020, https://www.rba.gov.au/publications/bulletin/2020/dec/long-term-unemployment-in-australia.html

Rejection

Job seeking is not easy. It takes time, and if you commit many hours each week to job seeking you will increase your chance of success and find work faster.

Treat job searching like a job by spending perhaps 25, 30 or 40 hours per week at it. Have a daily routine. Set small achievable and measurable goals. Take breaks when you need them. Take days off when you need. Socialise. Exercise. Continue with your hobbies and interests.

Find a mentor you can bounce ideas off and ask to review your job applications. Where possible, surround yourself with positive support people. Where you can't do this, try not to be dragged down by negativity. Realise that you aren't the only person searching for work. Accept that you're doing what you can to find work. Don't be too hard on yourself. Having one good networking contact with a person per day is a sign of a successful day.

Many job seekers become discouraged when they don't receive a response to their job application from an employer. Try not to become discouraged. Reframe employer feedback or lack of feedback as a learning opportunity that can feed into your decisions about changing your job search strategy (see the chapter 'Job search strategy').

Remember, when you access the hidden job market or even an advertised position, you are not asking for or begging for a job. You might be desperate for work, but you don't need to let the employer know this. What you're doing is offering an employer an opportunity to use and benefit from your experience, skills, and abilities. It's important to maintain a professional attitude rather than appear and act desperate for work, even if you feel desperate.

If an interview went well, keep job searching. Don't stop job searching while you wait for the job offer because if you don't get the offer, you will have lost a week or more in your job searching.

When economic times make it difficult to find work, some job seekers will still find work. When economic times make it easier to find work, there will be some job seekers who cannot find work, perhaps because they need to improve their job applications, interview skills, and/or access the hidden job market. So, don't be put off by how the economy is performing.

How to choose an occupation

Many readers will know their desired occupation. If this applies to you, then you may wish to skip to the next chapter. Keep reading if you don't know what occupation you want to work in or if you want to confirm your choice of occupation.

It's important to like the work you do because you probably need to work many hours per week and you may as well be happy doing it. For most people, interest is what drives choosing an occupation. However, for some people, values are the driver for choosing an occupation. Examples of values include wanting to earn a large salary, help people, or have a work/life balance.

Career assessments

What are your interests? The first step is to find out your interests, then match your interests to occupations. For people who are unsure of their interests, completing a career assessment may assist you. A career assessment will ask you some questions and, based on your answers, will provide a list of possible occupations and increase your self-awareness of your interests, values, skills, and abilities.

The world's most widely used career interest assessment tool is the Holland Self-Directed Search (SDS). This assessment may be completed online. It takes about 20 minutes to complete and is inexpensive. Alternatively, many countries have a government-run careers website where a free online career assessment can be completed. Some university websites offer free career assessments.

Unfortunately, no career assessment is 100% accurate or guaranteed to find the perfect occupation for you. However, career assessments may help you identify your career interests and occupations that you may find interesting. Sometimes career assessments suggest occupations that don't interest you. That's okay; they're not perfect.

Researching occupations

Once you have identified one or more possible occupations, learn more by reading occupational information on a government careers website. Watch videos of people who work in the occupation. Contact the relevant professional association and ask to speak with someone working in the occupation. You could contact people in the occupation by searching and connecting with them on LinkedIn, where you can see their career progression by browsing their employment history. Talk with people who are working in the occupation to get a better understanding of the work, possible career pathways, and how to enter the occupation. Another option to consider is shadowing someone working in the occupation to improve your understanding of the occupation. If training is required to work in the occupation, talk with the training course leader/trainer and/or alumni to better understand the career opportunities in the occupation.

While many occupations require a qualification, it might be possible to enter an occupation without a qualification. Ask people working in the occupation if entry to the occupation is possible without formal training. It may be possible to get a job in an occupation after starting training. If a person has transferable skills from another occupation, an employer may employ them without a qualification. Examples of transferable skills include communication, problem solving, and self-management.

The more research you do to find out about the occupation, the more likely your choice will be a good one. Spending little or no time researching the occupation may lead to a poor choice and lack of interest in the occupation, resulting in not completing the training or finding out the work is not like you thought it would be.

If having a list of occupations identified by a career assessment hasn't helped you find an occupation with which you could be happy, you may choose to:

- browse a list of occupations on a careers website and see if any interest you
- visit a career counsellor to assist you to decide on an occupation.

Values

It's important to consider your values when choosing an occupation. If you are a family person who values time spent on weekends with family, then real estate sales where you may need to work weekends is not for you. If helping people is important to you, working in a helping role, such as in health or education, is likely to be more satisfying than work that does not involve helping people.

Many people do work that does not interest them, but it pays the bills and in their spare time they have hobbies that interest them. However, it's better if you can find work that interests you and matches your values.

How to choose an occupation key points

- The driver for choosing an occupation for many people is interest, however some people are driven by values.

- If you are unsure of your interests, take a career assessment to become more aware of your interests, values, skills, and abilities.

- Investigate possible occupations by googling information about the occupation, watching videos, and speaking with people working in the occupation by contacting the relevant professional association or approaching them using LinkedIn.

- The more research you do, the less likely you are to make a poor decision.

Completing education to improve employment outcome

People with higher level qualifications generally have better employment outcomes than those who have not completed further training after leaving school.[109]

The effect of completing a Certificate III or IV

Job seekers without a post-school qualification who want to increase their chance of employment can do so by completing a Certificate III or IV. The normal caveats apply: ensure the course interests you (refer to the chapter 'How to choose an occupation') and is likely to lead to employment (refer to the chapter 'Labour market information').

The graph following[110] shows that the participation rate for people with a Certificate III or IV qualification is similar to those

---

109 Australian Government, Department of Jobs and Small Business, *Australian jobs 2021*, p. 44, https://www.nationalskillscommission.gov.au/sites/default/files/2021-10/NSC21-0025_Australian%20Jobs%202021_ACC-FA2.pdf

110 Australian Government, Department of Jobs and Small Business, *Australian jobs 2020*, https://www.nationalskillscommission.gov.au/sites/default/files/2020-11/Australian%20Jobs%20Report%202020.pdf

with a higher qualification. The participation rate is defined as the section of working population in the age group of 16–64 in the economy currently employed or seeking employment.[111]

Labour market outcomes by highest level of educational attainment, 2020 (%)

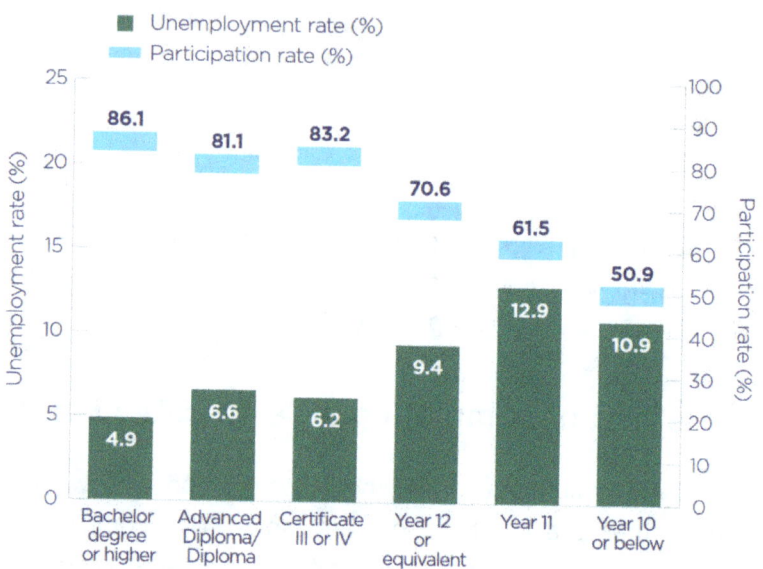

The effect of completing a master's degree

Graduates with a master's degree appear to be more employable.[112] However, some master's degrees may not make a person more employable. Graduates considering postgraduate studies need

---

111 'Definition of "Labour Force Participation Rate"', *The Economic Times*, https://economictimes.indiatimes.com/definition/labour-force-participation-rate
112 'Masters degrees & employability', *FindAMasters*, https://www.findamasters.com/advice/finding/masters-employability.aspx

to weigh the benefits with the cost and time the study would take.

Lower skilled occupations

Although most new jobs created in recent years (and those expected in the future) are in skilled occupations, there will continue to be large numbers of jobs in lower skilled occupations (that is, jobs which do not usually require post-school qualifications).

Lower skilled occupations generally have higher turnover rates than those that require post-school qualifications, with many job openings available each year across all industries.

Significant proportions of labourers (58%), sales workers (56%), and machinery operators and drivers (54%) do not hold post-school qualifications. This includes occupations like general sales assistants, waiters, checkout operators and office cashiers, and truck drivers. There are opportunities in all industries for people who do not have post-school qualifications. For example, more than half of the jobs in accommodation and food services and retail trade are held by workers who don't have such qualifications.[113]

Micro-credentials

Micro-credentials are mini-qualifications that demonstrate skills, knowledge, and/or experience in a given subject area or

---

113 Australian Government, National Skills Commission, *Australian jobs 2020*, p. 36, https://www.nationalskillscommission.gov.au/sites/default/files/2020-11/Australian%20Jobs%20Report%202020.pdf

capability. Also known as nanodegrees, micro-credentials tend to be narrower in range than traditional qualifications like diplomas or degrees. However, they can also be broad in focus rather than specific. For example, you can have a micro-credential for something as broad as data-driven marketing and another micro-credential focusing specifically on how to empower others in the workplace.[114]

Micro-credentials allow you to personalise your career development, broaden your resume, boost employability, and expand your options.[115]

> ## Completing education to improve employment outcome key points
>
> - People with higher level qualifications generally have better employment outcomes than those who have not completed further training after leaving school.[116]
> - Job seekers without a post-school qualification who want to increase their chance of employment can do so by completing a Certificate III or IV, assuming

---

114 'What are micro-credentials and how can they benefit both businesses and employees?', *DeakinCo.*, 24 October 2017, https://www.deakinco.com/media-centre/article/Benefits-of-micro-credentials-for-business-and-employees

115 'What are micro-credentials? And why are they important?', *RMIT Online*, 17 September 2020, https://online.rmit.edu.au/blog/what-are-micro-credentials-and-why-are-they-important

116 Australian Government, Department of Jobs and Small Business, *Australian jobs 2019*, p. 36, https://docs.employment.gov.au/system/files/doc/other/australianjobs2019.pdf

the course interests you and is likely to lead to employment.

- Graduates with a master's degree appear to be more employable.[117] However, some master's degrees may not make a person more employable.

- Although most new jobs will continue to be in skilled occupations, there will continue to be large numbers of jobs in lower skilled occupations, which do not usually require post-school qualifications.

- Micro-credentials are mini-qualifications that demonstrate skills, knowledge, and/or experience in a given subject area or capability.

- Micro-credentials allow you to personalise your career development, broaden your resume, boost employability, and expand your options.[118]

---

117 'Masters degrees & employability', *FindAMasters*, https://www.findamasters.com/advice/finding/masters-employability.aspx

118 'What are micro-credentials? And why are they important?', *RMIT Online*, 17 September 2020, https://online.rmit.edu.au/blog/what-are-micro-credentials-and-why-are-they-important

Changing occupations/ industries

When changing jobs, the following table summarises the options for changing your occupation and/or your industry.

Same occupation Same industry	Same occupation Different industry
Different occupation Same industry	Different occupation Different industry

Changing jobs from a programmer in a bank to a programmer in another bank is likely to be relatively easy because you are still in the same occupation and still in the same industry – banking. This situation is reflected in the top left-hand box in the table.

Changing jobs from a programmer in a bank to a programmer in the manufacturing or health industry could be expected to be more challenging than staying within banking but still doable. This situation is reflected in the top right-hand box in the table.

Changing from a programmer in the banking industry to another occupation in the banking industry is only possible within a company willing to retrain the programmer because the programmer would not be competitive against job seekers who already have qualifications/experience in that occupation. This situation is reflected in the bottom left-hand box in the table. An exception is where a programmer has completed training for another occupation, which would then enable the programmer to compete for entry-level jobs in the new occupation.

Changing to a different occupation and industry is the most difficult. The only exception is where a person changes to an entry-level job, e.g. a professional immigrant with poor language skills changes occupation to a cleaner. This situation is reflected in the bottom right-hand box in the table.

When a job seeker is changing their occupation, starting a training course displays a commitment and can strengthen their job applications by including the training on their resume, in their cover letters, and in responses to selection criteria.

Consider a functional resume format when changing occupation. See the 'Resume format' section in the 'Resume writing' chapter.

Labour market information

Labour market information may be defined as 'Information related to conditions in, or the operation of the labour market, including wages, job openings, working conditions, and current and future skill, occupation and industry requirements'.[119]

The role of labour market information in choosing an occupation

The employment outlook for an occupation should not be the primary or sole career decision-making criterion. Other factors such as interests and values should be the primary career decision-making criteria. Labour market information can be a factor in choosing an occupation. The problem with choosing an occupation based on labour market information such as employment outlook or salary is that working in an occupation that does not interest you or that contradicts your values is likely to cause you to cease working or to be unhappy at work.

If you are qualified and/or experienced in more than one occupation, looking at the labour market statistics for each occupation may influence which occupation to focus on in your job

---

[119] Australian Government Department of Education, Employment and Workplace Relations. Ministerial Council for Education, Early Childhood Development and Youth Affairs. *Australian blueprint for career development*, 2010. https://cica.org.au/wp-content/uploads/Australian-Blueprint-for-Career-Development.pdf

search. The employment outlook within an occupation can vary. For example, there might be a shortage of mining engineers in a remote mining location and an oversupply in a city. Also, there might be a shortage of surgical nurses and an oversupply for graduate nurses. Data at this level is not collected or available.

The role of labour market information in job seeking

So, how can labour market information help with job seeking?

Let's look at industries. Industries are groups of organisations based on their business activities and include education, manufacturing, health and construction, to name a few.[120] Most people know what occupation they want to do but may not be aware of the range of industries that employ people in that occupation. For example, a receptionist may work in a manufacturing company, a transportation company, or a health company. Receptionists are employed in every industry.

Currently in developed countries, employment in the health care and social assistance industry is projected to grow strongly whereas employment in manufacturing is projected to fall. The key message is that a job may be easier to obtain in a faster growing industry than a slower growing or declining industry. You need to be careful with broad generalisations as, for example, in the primary metal and metal product manufacturing sector growth of 6,400 (or 8.5 per cent) is projected.[121] So, it's important to look at the statistics for each part of each industry.

---

120 Industry definition, *Investopedia*. https://www.investopedia.com/terms/i/industry.asp
121 Australian Government, '2020 Industry Employment Outlook (Word)', p. 5, *Labour Market Information Portal*, https://lmip.gov.au/default.aspx?LMIP/GainInsights/EmploymentProjections

Labour market information for each occupation should be provided on your government's careers website. Locating industry labour market information may require more research. Industry labour market information may also be available on your government's careers website but you may need to look at a government labour market information website or a government employment website.

Governments maintain labour market information in databases available to the public. Contact the area of government responsible for labour market information to learn how to access these databases. You can find the major industries that employ your occupation by searching a government database containing occupation and industry labour market information. Find the industry code for each industry by searching online for 'list of industry codes'. Once you've obtained the major industry codes for your occupation you can search a business database using industry code as a search parameter to view a list of companies that operate in that industry. You can access a business database at your local or regional library. Library members might be able to access a business database remotely depending on library policy. The list of companies operating in that industry can then be approached as part of your hidden job market search.

The effect of automation on the future of the workforce

Regarding automation and the future of the workforce over the next 10 years, the need for some skills, such as technological as well as social and emotional skills, will rise, even as the demand for others, including physical and manual skills, will fall.[122] Occupations that require technological, social, creative, and/or emotional skills will be less likely to be affected by automation.

> ## Labour market information key points
>
> - Labour market information may be a consideration but should not be the prime or sole factor in choosing an occupation.
> - It may be easier to find work in industries that are growing rather than declining.
> - Labour market information about industries is available from government and/or careers websites.
> - Labour market information can identify which industries employ the most people in an occupation. Companies in those industries can be targeted for hidden market job seeking.
> - For job seekers concerned about the future of work, occupations which require technological, social, creative, and emotional skills will be less affected by automation.

---

122 J Bughin et al., 'Skill shift: automation and the future of the workforce', *McKinsey & Company*, 23 May 2018, https://www.mckinsey.com/featured-insights/future-of-work/skill-shift-automation-and-the-future-of-the-workforce

Social media

HR professionals/recruiters may look at a job seeker's social media profiles and posts before extending a job offer. A study found that 45% of hiring managers use social media to gain insight on applicants. Seventy per cent of those surveyed said they had rejected an applicant because of things discovered on their applicant's social media.[123] Inappropriate photos and/or posts might rule you out of contention for a job. Review your social media profiles to make changes/deletions if necessary. Google your name to check for any inappropriate content.

Usage of social media for job advertisements is rising rapidly. Platforms such as Facebook now allow employers and job seekers to interact through region-based job groups.[124]

---

123 Wikipedia, 'Artificial intelligence in hiring', *Wikipedia, the Free Encyclopedia*, updated 6 December 2021, https://en.wikipedia.org/wiki/Artificial_intelligence_in_hiring; P Holland & D Jeske, 2017, *Changing role of social media at work: implications for recruitment and selection*, Electronic HRM in the Smart Era, Emerald Publishing Limited, pp. 287–309

124 Australian Government, Department of Jobs and Small Business, *Australian jobs 2019*, https://cica.org.au/wp-content/uploads/Australian-Jobs-Snapshot-2019.pdf

Personal branding

Your personal brand is essentially marketing yourself and your career expertise. It signals what you stand for, what you've accomplished, and what you're capable of achieving.

Having a personal brand can provide you with many benefits when it comes to finding a new job and staying relevant in your career.[125] Benefits include being authentic, gains in confidence, building credibility, showcasing your speciality, connection to your audience and distinguishing yourself from your competition.[126]

How to define your personal brand

Start by identifying your short-term and long-term goals. Identify anything that prevents you from attaining your goals. Identify what you need to attain your goals such as training. Identify your strengths through introspection and speaking with colleagues. Identify your personal characteristics that differentiate you from your colleagues through introspection and asking colleagues for their views.

---

125 C Lock, 'How to create a personal brand that enhances your job search', *FlexJobs*, https://www.flexjobs.com/blog/post/how-to-create-a-personal-brand-to-enhance-your-job-search-v2/
126 S Chritton, 'Ten key benefits of personal branding', *Dummies*, https://www.dummies.com/careers/find-a-job/personal-branding/ten-key-benefits-of-personal-branding/

How to write a personal branding statement

You can summarise your personal brand in a 1–2 sentence statement that clearly tells people who you are and what you stand for. It's a quick way for people to know what it is that makes the brand that is you so important and unique and helps to clearly state what it is you represent.[127]

One way to come up with a personal branding statement is to ensure it includes:

- your specialty – who you are
- your service – what you do
- your audience – who you do it for
- your best characteristics – what you're known for
- your best accomplishments – what your track record proves.[128]

Example personal branding statement:

International digital marketing specialist who's launched over 20 websites in 10 languages across 12 countries. Now looking for an exciting opportunity to combine my technical and creative marketing capabilities, ideally in the ecommerce or B2B space.[129]

---

127 M Simpson, 'Personal branding for job seekers 101', *The Interview Guys*, https://theinterviewguys.com/personal-branding-for-job-seekers-101/

128 JL Kennedy, 'How to create a personal brand for your job search', *Dummies*, https://www.dummies.com/careers/find-a-job/how-to-create-a-personal-brand-for-your-job-search/

129 'Top tips for a killer personal brand statement', *Robert Walters Group*, https://www.robertwaltersgroup.com/news/expert-insight/careers-blog/how-to-write-a-personal-brand-statement.html

You're now ready to write a personable branding statement. Your personal brand needs to be consistent across social media and your job applications, interviews, and networking.

> ## Personal branding key points
>
> - Your personal brand is essentially marketing yourself and your career expertise.
> - It's a quick way for people to know what it is that makes the brand that is you so important and unique and helps to clearly state what it is you represent.[130]
> - Identify your personal characteristics that differentiate you from your colleagues through introspection and asking colleagues for their views.
> - Make your personal brand consistent across social media and your job applications, interviews, and networking.

---

[130] M Simpson, 'Personal branding for job seekers 101', *The Interview Guys*, https://theinterviewguys.com/personal-branding-for-job-seekers-101/

Job clubs

A job club is a group of job seekers who meet regularly to support each other in job seeking.

Joining a job club can provide many benefits:

- Get assistance with your job applications.
- Practise your interview skills.
- Network with attendees.
- Peer support.
- Provide structure to your job seeking, i.e. regular meetings.

You can set up or access a job club via social media. Here you can find or build groups that organise online events or host in-person events for people with similar interests.

Government employment services providers

Employment services providers assist job seekers to find work. In Australia, government-contracted employment services providers are graded on their performance at getting people into work. Every three months each branch receives a star rating. One star is the lowest performing and five stars is the best performing. So, if you want to find work go to a five-star branch. However, it is possible that staff at five-star branches lean on job seekers to take jobs they don't want due to the pressure to get high star ratings. So, perhaps search for a three-star or four-star company instead.

The number of stars for each branch of each company is available via the Australian Government Department of Education, Skills and Employment website for Workforce Australia employment services providers and Australian Government Department of Social Services for Disability Employment Services providers.[131]

---

131 Australian Government, Department of Education Skills and Employment, 'jobactive Star Ratings and performance', *jobactive*, https://www.dese.gov.au/jobactive/jobactive-star-ratings-and-performance ; Australian Government, Department of Social Services, 'Published DES Star ratings', *Disability and Carers*, https://www.dss.gov.au/disability-and-carers-programs-services-disability-employment-services/published-des-star-ratings

If you are not happy with your assigned employment consultant at your employment services provider, ask to change consultants. If you are not happy with your employment services provider, request a transfer to another provider.

Volunteering

Volunteer roles have numerous benefits for the job seeker.

They allow you to:

- participate in the community
- improve your mental health
- learn new skills
- gain a referee
- enhance your resume
- meet people who may know of job openings
- grow your network of contacts
- find work (in rare cases).

You may want to limit the number of hours per week you volunteer to avoid compromising the time spent job searching.

You can pick and choose what volunteer role(s) you want. Ideally, choose something that enhances your experience and makes it easier for you to find work. Even if you volunteer in a field that does not enhance your experience, the role may develop or hone your employability skills (see the 'Employability skills' section in the 'Resume writing' chapter).

Within a volunteer role, a volunteer may be able to choose the duties they would like to do if the volunteer coordinator is agreeable.

Artificial intelligence in hiring

It is increasingly common for companies to use Artificial intelligence (AI) to automate aspects of their hiring process.

Advances in artificial intelligence, such as the advent of machine learning and the growth of big data, enable AI to be utilised to recruit, screen, and predict the success of applicants. Proponents of artificial intelligence in hiring claim it reduces bias, assists with finding qualified candidates, and frees up human resource workers' time for other tasks, while opponents worry that AI perpetuates inequalities in the workplace and will eliminate jobs.[132]

The author believes that the best way to prepare for AI in the hiring process is to follow the strategies in this book.

---

132 Wikipedia, 'Artificial intelligence in hiring', *Wikipedia, the Free Encyclopedia*, updated 6 December 2021, https://en.wikipedia.org/wiki/Artificial_intelligence_in_hiring

Chatbots

Recruitment chatbots[133] are conversational interface platforms that perform the preliminary recruitment process. They are powered with AI and Natural Language Processing capabilities.

Chatbots can

- Screen candidate applications
  - Once candidates apply on a company's job site, chatbots ask them questions, such as work experience, previous company details, interest areas, etc. Assessing the job requirement[s], the conversation and resume details, the recruitment chatbot can decide whether a candidate fits the job or not.

- Schedule interviews
  - Chatbots can schedule an interview date and time for relevant candidates.

- Answer queries
  - Chatbots can instantly answer candidates' questions about the job, work environment, and salary structure.

Problems recruitment chatbots may encounter

- Lack of empathy

---

133 N Joshi, 'Recruitment chatbots: is the hype worth it?', *Forbes*, https://www.forbes.com/sites/cognitiveworld/2019/02/09/recruitment-chatbot-is-the-hype-worth-it/?sh=7f4a27204083

- Language barrier
    - Some might prefer abbreviations while some might like the conversation to be formal. Some chatbots may not understand the difference.
- Decision-making capabilities
    - AI chatbots are meant to learn from previous conversations but can fall short in places where they have to make decisions on their own.

Recommendations when conversing with chatbots

- Don't use abbreviations.
- Don't use sarcasm.
- Don't use slang.
- Try not to use answers that have even a hint of ambiguity.

Artificial intelligence key points

- AI is being used to automate recruiting, screening, and predicting the success of candidates.
- Following the strategies laid out in this book, such as interview skills, selection criteria responses, resume and cover letter preparation, is the best way to prepare for AI in hiring.
- Recruitment chatbots are conversational interface platforms that perform the preliminary recruitment process.

- Some chatbots may not understand abbreviations, slang, use of sarcasm, or ambiguous answers that could be misinterpreted.

Conclusion

Many job seekers limit themselves to applying for advertised jobs on the internet using the same resume and cover letter. They don't change their job search strategy even if they haven't been getting interviews.

Job seekers who tailor their resume and cover letters to the job ad and write key selection criteria using the STAR framework are more likely to be successful in getting interviews. Preparing for likely interview questions can improve performance at interviews.

19% of jobs are 'hidden' or never advertised.[134] They can be accessed by directly approaching employers even if they currently have no job openings and by networking with family, friends, and colleagues who may know of job openings.

If you find yourself struggling to find work, reach out to friends who work in HR or recruitment or contact a career counsellor for advice and assistance.

Treat job hunting like a job. Put in the time and effort it deserves. You'll likely find work faster and avoid mental health issues. Be kind to yourself and surround yourself with positive, supportive people.

Good luck in your job hunting!

---

134 Australian Government, National Skills Commission, *Survey of employers' recruitment experiences: 2019 data report*, https://lmip.gov.au/PortalFile.axd?FieldID=3193776&.pdf

Appendix A: Functional resume template

Name
Address
Phone
Email

Career Summary

Skills

Skill 1
Demonstrate where you learned or honed the skill (example one)
Demonstrate where you learned or honed the skill (example two)
Demonstrate where you learned or honed the skill (example three)

Skill 2
Demonstrate where you learned or honed the skill (example one)
Demonstrate where you learned or honed the skill (example two)
Demonstrate where you learned or honed the skill (example three)

Education

Work History

Job title	Dates
Company	
Job title	Dates
Company	

Volunteer roles

Interests

Appendix B: Reverse chronological resume template

Name
Address
Phone
Email

Career Summary

Skills

Work History

Job title   Dates
Company
Duties

Job title   Dates
Company
Duties

Education

Volunteer roles

Interests

Appendix C: Combination resume template

Name
Address
Phone
Email

Career Summary

Skills

Skill 1
Demonstrate where you learned or honed the skill (example one)
Demonstrate where you learned or honed the skill (example two)
Demonstrate where you learned or honed the skill (example three)

Skill 2
Demonstrate where you learned or honed the skill (example one)
Demonstrate where you learned or honed the skill (example two)
Demonstrate where you learned or honed the skill (example three)

Work History

Job title   Dates
Company
Duties

Job title   Dates
Company
Duties

Education

Volunteer roles

Interests

Appendix D: Work history summary for your referees

Name: <your name>   Job title: <your job title>

Start date:
End date:

Duties:

Strengths:
1.
2.
3.

Weakness:
1.

Accomplishments:

Types of work you are looking for:

Appendix E: T-Bar cover letter template

Dear <first name>,

I am excited to apply for the position of Accountant, Job Ref 2276, advertised on your website. I am attaching this cover letter and my resume for your perusal.

Below I have outlined my qualifications to address your stated requirements.

Your job requirements	My experience
1st job requirement	Response to 1st job requirement
2nd job requirement	Response to 2nd job requirement

I would welcome the opportunity to meet with you personally at an interview to provide you with further details of my qualifications and professional skills in relation to this application. I can be contacted on ....

Yours sincerely,

<your name>

Appendix F: T-Bar cover letter template

Dear <first name>,

I am excited to apply for the position of Accountant, Job Ref 2276, advertised on your website. I am attaching this cover letter and my resume for your perusal.

Below I have outlined my qualifications to address your stated requirements.

1st job requirement
Response to 1st job requirement

2nd job requirement
Response to 2nd job requirement

etc.

I would welcome the opportunity to meet with you personally at an interview to provide you with further details of my qualifications and professional skills in relation to this application. I can be contacted on ....

Yours sincerely,

<your name>

Appendix G: Marketing email template

Dear <first name>,

State your name and occupation. If you are not currently working in the field, you can say that you hope to gain work in <occupation>. Say how you knew to contact the person (LinkedIn, Professional association, another contact).

Explain why you are writing to the person. Do not ask them for a job.

Briefly provide your relevant background (qualifications, experience, transferable skills).

Thank the person for their time and say you will contact them to set up a meeting time.

Yours sincerely,

<your name>

Appendix H: Marketing email example for someone not changing fields

Dear <first name>,

I note with interest your company's activities as described on your website.

I've been in engineering for five years and I'm currently exploring new opportunities in the mining industry. As such, I thought you would be an excellent contact for me to find out more about the industry. I want to emphasise that I am gathering information currently in my job search and am writing for advice regarding this industry. I do not expect you to know of any job opportunities.

I received a Bachelor of Engineering from The University of Melbourne, and I immediately entered BHPs training program. Within five years I was a supervisor.

Your thoughts and ideas regarding this industry would be most helpful.

I hope it will be possible for us to meet and I will phone you later in the week to arrange a mutually convenient time.

Yours sincerely,

<your name>

Appendix I: Marketing email example for someone changing fields

Dear <first name>,

I note with interest your company's activities as described on your website.

I am currently a receptionist, however I am researching the medical reception industry and thought you would be an excellent contact for me to find out more about the industry. I see this industry as a natural career progression step. I want to emphasise that I am writing for advice that will help me in my job search in this industry and do not expect you to know of any job opportunities. Your thoughts and ideas would be most helpful.

I have three years' experience working as a nurse and four years as a receptionist. My excellent verbal and written communication skills matched with my personality and life experiences enable exceptional rapport with patients. I would be interested to hear your views on how my background might fit into your industry.

I hope it will be possible for us to meet and I will phone you later in the week to arrange a mutually convenient time.

Yours sincerely,

<your name>

Appendix J: Disability disclosure chart

The following chart was an internal document of the now defunct CRS Australia, a leading provider of disability employment and assessment services to people with a disability, injury or health condition. This chart was revised from the 'Epilepsy Disclosure Chart' by Disability Resources Inc.

Time of disclosure	Advantages	Disadvantages	Issues
ON A JOB APPLICATION:	• Appears honest. • Have peace of mind. • Lets employer decide if disability is an issue.	• Risk of discrimination. • May decrease chance to present skills/ explain effects of disability. • No comeback.	• May have a harder time finding work but usually have a more supportive workplace when you do.
DURING AN INTERVIEW:	• Appears honest. • Have peace of mind. • Chance to explain effects of disability positively in person. • Discrimination less likely face to face.	• May not get job offer. • May change focus from your abilities to your disability. • You may not handle disability issues in a clear/ non-threatening way.	• How comfortable are you with discussing your disability? • Are you emphasising your disability too much?

Time of disclosure	Advantages	Disadvantages	Issues
AFTER THE INTERVIEW: (When job is offered but before you begin work)	• Appears honest. • Have peace of mind. • If employer changes mind after disclosure and you are sure your disability will not interfere with your ability to perform the job, or job safety, there may be legal comeback.	• Employer might feel you should have told them before the decision was made. Might lead to distrust of you.	• Need to look honestly at how disability affects ability to perform tasks of the job. Need to be able to explain how disability will not interfere. This includes job safety.
AFTER YOU START WORK:	• Opportunity to prove yourself before disclosure. • Allows you to answer workmate's questions. • If disclosure affects employment status and your condition will not interfere with your ability to perform the job, or job safety, you may be protected by law against dismissal.	• Employer may feel you have falsified application. • You may feel nervous and afraid of relapse on the job. • Co-workers may not know how to react if you become unwell. • You may be treated differently from other staff, e.g. given simpler tasks.	• The longer you leave the disclosure, the harder it becomes. • It may be difficult to know who to tell.

Time of disclosure	Advantages	Disadvantages	Issues
NEVER:	• Employer cannot react to your disability unless you have a relapse which affects your work performance.	• If your disability is discovered and it potentially affects work performance/safety, you run the risk of being fired. • May not get the support you need when it is required. • Increased stress from fear of being 'found out'.	• If you have not had a relapse for a long time, the issue of disclosure becomes less critical.

Appendix K: Percentage of recruiting employers who did not advertise by occupation

ANZSCO 1 digit Occupation	% recruiting employers* who did not advertise
Clerical and Administrative Workers	20%
Community and Personal Service Workers	16%
Labourers	25%
Machinery Operators and Drivers	23%
Managers	17%
Professionals	15%
Sales Workers	24%
Technicians and Trades Workers	21%

* Recruiting employers are employers who were currently recruiting or who had recruited in the previous month

Source: Australian Government, Department of Education, Skills and Employment, 'Recruitment and Employer Needs Analysis', Labour Market Research and Analysis Branch, *National Skills Commission*.

ANZSCO is the Australian and New Zealand Standard Classification of Occupations. The structure of ANZSCO has five hierarchical levels. The lowest level are termed 'occupations'.[135]

---

[135] Australian Bureau of Statistics, 'Conceptual basis of ANZSCO', *ABS website*, https://www.abs.gov.au/statistics/classifications/anzsco-australian-and-new-zealand-standard-classification-occupations/2021/conceptual-basis-anzsco

ANZSCO 2 digit Occupation	% recruiting employers* who did not advertise
Automotive and Engineering Trades Workers	23%
Business, Human Resource and Marketing Professionals	19%
Carers and Aides	10%
Cleaners and Laundry Workers	17%
Construction and Mining Labourers	29%
Construction Trades Workers	27%
Design, Engineering, Science and Transport Professionals	15%
Education Professionals	8%
Electrotechnology and Telecommunications Trades Workers	30%
Engineering, ICT and Science Technicians	15%
Factory Process Workers	27%
Farm, Forestry and Garden Workers	22%**
Food Preparation Assistants	23%
Food Trades Workers	13%
General Clerical Workers	21%
Health Professionals	15%
Hospitality Workers	22%
Hospitality, Retail and Service Managers	7%**
Inquiry Clerks and Receptionists	21%
Legal, Social and Welfare Professionals	15%**
Machine and Stationary Plant Operators	22%**
Mobile Plant Operators	32%**
Numerical Clerks	16%**
Other Clerical and Administrative Workers	18%**
Other Labourers	30%

ANZSCO 2 digit Occupation	% recruiting employers* who did not advertise
Other Technicians and Trades Workers	16%
Road and Rail Drivers	21%
Sales Assistants and Salespersons	24%
Sales Representatives and Agents	21%
Sales Support Workers	30%
Skilled Animal and Horticultural Workers	15%**
Specialist Managers	21%
Sports and Personal Service Workers	19%**
Storepersons	22%

* Recruiting employers are employers who were currently recruiting or who had recruited in the previous month

** Based on low number of records and should be treated with caution

HOW TO FIND A JOB

ANZSCO 3 digit Occupation	% recruiting employers* who did not advertise
Accountants, Auditors and Company Secretaries	23%**
Accounting Clerks and Bookkeepers	18%**
Architects, Designers, Planners and Surveyors	24%**
Automotive Electricians and Mechanics	27%
Bricklayers, and Carpenters and Joiners	31%**
Building and Engineering Technicians	17%**
Checkout Operators and Office Cashiers	28%
Child Carers	9%
Cleaners and Laundry Workers	17%
Construction and Mining Labourers	29%
Construction, Distribution and Production Managers	20%**
Delivery Drivers	21%**
Electricians	33%**
Electronics and Telecommunications Trades Workers	25%**
Engineering Professionals	10%**
Fabrication Engineering Trades Workers	19%
Farm, Forestry and Garden Workers	22%**
Food Preparation Assistants	23%
Food Process Workers	26%**
Food Trades Workers	13%
General Clerks	21%
Hospitality Workers	22%
Insurance Agents and Sales Representatives	16%**
Machine Operators	20%**
Mechanical Engineering Trades Workers	18%**
Midwifery and Nursing Professionals	18%**

ANZSCO 3 digit Occupation	% recruiting employers* who did not advertise
Miscellaneous Factory Process Workers	29%
Miscellaneous Labourers	28%
Mobile Plant Operators	32%**
Natural and Physical Science Professionals	8%**
Personal Carers and Assistants	9%
Plumbers	22%**
Real Estate Sales Agents	26%**
Receptionists	23%
Sales Assistants and Salespersons	24%
School Teachers	6%
Storepersons	22%
Truck Drivers	21%
Wood Trades Workers	12%**

* Recruiting employers are employers who were currently recruiting or who had recruited in the previous month

** Based on low number of records and should be treated with caution

Appendix L: Percentage of recruiting employers who did not advertise by industry

ANZSCO 1 digit Industry	% recruiting employers* who did not advertise
Accommodation and Food Services	18%
Administrative and Support Services	10%
Agriculture, Forestry and Fishing	26%
Arts and Recreation Services	23%
Construction	25%
Education and Training	17%
Financial and Insurance Services	11%**
Health Care and Social Assistance	12%
Manufacturing	23%
Other Services	25%
Professional, Scientific and Technical Services	18%
Rental, Hiring and Real Estate Services	24%
Retail Trade	26%
Transport, Postal and Warehousing	26%
Wholesale Trade	21%

* Recruiting employers are employers who were currently recruiting or who had recruited in the previous month

** Based on low number of records and should be treated with caution

Source: Australian Government, Department of Education, Skills and Employment, 'Recruitment and Employer Needs Analysis', Labour Market Research and Analysis Branch, *National Skills Commission*.

The ANZSIC is the Australian and New Zealand Standard Industrial Classification. The ANZSIC is a hierarchical classification with four levels.[136]

---

[136] Australian Bureau of Statistics, 1292.0 – Australian and New Zealand Standard Industrial Classification (ANZSIC), 2006, (Revision 2.0), updated 26 June 2013, https://www.abs.gov.au/ausstats/abs@.nsf/Latestproducts/39C6552D10C40EB1CA257B9500133CFA?opendocument

HOW TO FIND A JOB

ANZSCO 2 digit Industry	% recruiting employers* who did not advertise
Accommodation	19%
Agriculture	25%**
Basic Material Wholesaling	15%
Building Cleaning, Pest Control and Other Support Services	8%**
Building Construction	22%
Construction Services	26%
Fabricated Metal Product Manufacturing	20%
Food and Beverage Services	17%
Food Product Manufacturing	30%
Food Retailing	31%
Fuel Retailing	26%**
Grocery, Liquor and Tobacco Product Wholesaling	24%**
Heavy and Civil Engineering Construction	24%**
Machinery and Equipment Manufacturing	20%
Machinery and Equipment Wholesaling	20%
Medical and Other Health Care Services	18%
Motor Vehicle and Motor Vehicle Parts Retailing	17%
Non-Metallic Mineral Product Manufacturing	30%**
Other Store-Based Retailing	26%
Personal and Other Services	21%**
Preschool and School Education	15%
Professional, Scientific and Technical Services (Except Computer System Design and Related Services)	19%
Property Operators and Real Estate Services	27%
Repair and Maintenance	28%
Residential Care Services	20%

ANZSCO 2 digit Industry	% recruiting employers* who did not advertise
Road Transport	28%
Social Assistance Services	7%
Sports and Recreation Activities	24%**
Transport Equipment Manufacturing	17%**
Wood Product Manufacturing	22%**

* Recruiting employers are employers who were currently recruiting or who had recruited in the previous month

** Based on low number of records and should be treated with caution

ANZSCO 3 digit Industry	% recruiting employers* who did not advertise
Accommodation	19%
Allied Health Services	14%
Architectural, Engineering and Technical Services	20%
Automotive Repair and Maintenance	26%
Bakery Product Manufacturing	28%
Building Cleaning, Pest Control and Gardening Services	6%**
Building Completion Services	27%**
Building Installation Services	26%
Cafes, Restaurants and Takeaway Food Services	16%
Child Care Services	7%
Clothing, Footwear and Personal Accessory Retailing	25%**
Clubs (Hospitality)	26%**
Fuel Retailing	26%**
Grocery, Liquor and Tobacco Product Wholesaling	24%**
Hardware, Building and Garden Supplies Retailing	25%**
Heavy and Civil Engineering Construction	24%**
Legal and Accounting Services	21%
Medical Services	22%
Motor Vehicle Parts and Tyre Retailing	15%**
Motor Vehicle Retailing	18%**
Non-Residential Building Construction	13%**
Other Construction Services	16%**
Other Machinery and Equipment Wholesaling	17%**
Other Social Assistance Services	8%**
Other Wood Product Manufacturing	22%**
Pharmaceutical and Other Store-Based Retailing	23%

ANZSCO 3 digit Industry	% recruiting employers* who did not advertise
Preschool Education	17%**
Pubs, Taverns and Bars	18%
Real Estate Services	27%
Recreational Goods Retailing	45%**
Residential Building Construction	28%**
Residential Care Services	20%
Road Freight Transport	29%**
School Education	12%
Specialised Food Retailing	23%**
Specialised Industrial Machinery and Equipment Wholesaling	25%**
Specialised Machinery and Equipment Manufacturing	21%**
Sports and Physical Recreation Activities	27%**
Structural Metal Product Manufacturing	20%
Supermarket and Grocery Stores	36%
Timber and Hardware Goods Wholesaling	19%**
Veterinary Services	17%**

* Recruiting employers are employers who were currently recruiting or who had recruited in the previous month

** Based on low number of records and should be treated with caution

Index

A

accomplishment statements 27–28
    examples 28
artificial intelligence in hiring 237–240
    chatbots 238–239
assessment centres 157–161
    what happens 157
    what you need to do 158–160
automated resume scanning software 53–54
    trying to beat the Automated Tracking System 53
awards 34

B

Behavioural Event Interview (BEI) questions 132–136
    how to answer a BEI question when you don't have an example 136
    sample BEI question and answer 133–134

C

career summary 16–19
    examples 17–19
combination resume 44, 48–51
combination resume template 245–246
cover letters 61–68
    concluding paragraph 62–63
    first paragraph 62
    including quotes 63
    letter structure 61–62
    middle paragraphs 62
    pronouns 14–15
    salutation 62
    T-Bar cover letter 63–68
    templates 248–249
curriculum vitae 39
Customised Employment 185
criminal record 150–151

D

disability employment 183–187
    consider disclosing your disability 183
    how to disclose your disability at an interview 184
    Customised Employment 185
    disclosure chart 253–255
    supported employment 186
    Supported Wage System 184–185
    workplace modifications 184
duties 24–27

E

education 32–33
    which qualifications to include 32–33
    including/excluding 36
employment history 22–31

accomplishment statements 27–28
    examples 28
company description 23
dates alignment 30–31
duties 24–27
example 23
formatting multiple roles in the one company 28–29
power verbs 25–27
preventing the 'job hopper' look 31
relevant employment history 29–30
employment services providers 101, 233–234
employment summary 22

F
foreign names 13, 196–197
functional resume template 243

G
gaps in your resume 42–43
gig economy 181
graduate resume 37–38
graduate student employment 191–192

H
headline, LinkedIn 111
headline, resume 16
hidden job market 81–98
    accessing hidden job market jobs 82–83
    approaching employers 84–85
    best way to contact employers 85–86
        dropping off a resume in person 86
        emailing a hiring manager 91–92
        finding the hiring manager's name 88
        phoning 86–87
        phoning a hiring manager 88–91
        speaking with the hiring manager 87–91
    boomerang employee 97
    definition 81
    informational interviews 92–96
        elevator speech 96
        objectives 93–94
        questions 94–95
    networking 83
    searching a business database to find companies in your industry 85
holiday/part-time student resume 38

I
immigrants 195–200
    applying for work before arriving in your new country 195
    job seeking after immigration 195–199
        changing your resume to avoid discrimination 198
        difficulty finding work 197
        having to change occupation 197–198
        job applications and work culture differences between countries 199
        lack of local experience 197
        language 196
        networking 196–197
        overseas referees 199
        recognition of overseas qualifications 195–196
interests 34–35
interviews 123–153

answering Behavioural Event
    Interview (BEI) questions
    132–136
    answering a BEI question
        when you don't have an
        example 136
    sample BEI question and
        answer 133–134
asking questions of the
    interviewers 136–138
clothes 124–125
feedback 155–156
digital 140–141
dining 141–142
general tips 144–152
    accepting a drink 146
    answering difficult
        questions 147
    criminal record 150–151
    how graduates can answer
        questions about their
        experience 148
    how to know if you are giving
        the right answer 146
    humour 152
    illegal questions 148–150
    managing nervousness 145
    reception area
        etiquette 145–146
    running late 146
    sending a thank you email
        after an interview 152
    what to do if you don't know
        the answer to a
        question 147
group 142–143
how to end the interview 138–139
likely questions 126–132
panel 144
preparation 123

researching if a company is a good
    place to work 125
scheduling 125–126
second interview 139
sickness 126
video 139–140

J

job applications 77–80
    follow up 79
    feedback 79
    forms 77–78
        salary field 78
        where to apply 78
    late applications 77
    when to apply 77
job search strategy 99–104
    changing an unsuccessful
        strategy 103
    job clubs 231
    job search intervention 102
    uploading your resume to a job
        board/employer employment
        register 102–103
    where to spend your job seeking
        time based on labour market
        information 100–101
job search troubleshooting 3–11
    job seeking methods 5
    typical mistakes and how to
        correct them 6–10
        cover letters 8
        interviews 9
        job search strategy 9–10
        key selection criteria 8
        phone voice mail messages 8
        resume 6–7
job seeker overqualified 171–172
job seeker underqualified 173–174
job seeking in another state 189
job seeking in the gig economy 181

job seeking when you're employed 179–180

K

key selection criteria 69–75
    definition 69
    STAR framework 70–71
    STAR response tips 72

L

labour market information 221–224
    effect of automation on the future of the workforce 223–224
    role of labour market information in choosing an occupation 221–222
    role of labour market information in job seeking 222–223
languages 45
LinkedIn as a job search tool 105–112
    applying for jobs using 'Easy apply' or 'Apply' 109
    headline 111
    how LinkedIn can assist your job search 108
    networking using LinkedIn 110–111
    privacy concerns 105–107
    starting to use 107–108
    search engine optimisation 109
    subscribing to LinkedIn premium 111
LinkedIn hyperlink 15
long-term unemployment 201–206
    how to get a job after long-term unemployment 201–204
    tips for finding a job after long-term unemployment 204–205

M

marketing email example for job seeker changing fields 252
marketing email example for job seeker not changing fields 251
marketing email template 250
maternity leave 44
mature age job seekers 175–176
multiple job offers 169

N

networking for hidden job market jobs 83
networking for immigrants 196–197
networking using LinkedIn 110–111

O

occupation choosing 209–212
    career assessments 209–210
    researching occupations 210–211
    values 211–212
overqualified job seeker 171–172
overseas qualifications 195–196

P

percentage of recruiting employers who did not advertise by industry 261–266
percentage of recruiting employers who did not advertise by occupation 256–260
personal branding 227–229
    defining your personal brand 227
    writing a personal branding statement 228–229
phone screening interviews 119–121
    phone interview feedback 121
phoning the job advertiser 59–60
power verbs 25–27
professional year programs 193–194
pronouns 14–15
psychometric testing 163–164
    tips 164

R

recognition of overseas qualifications 195–196
recruitment agencies 113–118
    how to choose 113–114
    managing a relationship with a recruiter 114–117
    salary discussion 117–118
recruitment methods employers use 4–5
referees 35, 55–58
    overseas referees 199
    resume format 35
    what to do if you don't have any referees 56–57
    written references 57
rejection 207–208
resume format 43–44
    functional 43, template 243
    reverse chronological 43, template 244
    combination 44, template 245–246
resume writing 13–51
    awards 34
    career summary 16–17
        examples 17–19
    curriculum vitae 39
    email address 15
    education 32
        which qualifications to include 32–33
        including/excluding 36
    employment history 22–31
        accomplishment statements 27–28
            examples 28
        company description 23
        dates alignment 30–31
        duties 24–27
        example 23
        formatting multiple roles in the one company 28–29
        power verbs 25–27
        preventing the 'job hopper' look 31
        relevant employment history 29–30
    employment summary 22
    foreign names 13, 196–197
    graduate resume 37–38
    headline 16
    holiday/part-time student resume 38
    home address 15
    interests 34–35
    LinkedIn hyperlink 15
    name and contact details 13
    professional memberships 33
    pronouns 14–15
    referees 35
    skills 19–22
        examples 19–21
        employability skills 21–22
        hard 19
        soft 19
    training 33
    unisex names 14
    volunteer roles 33–34
    general resume tips 39–50
        defining terms 41
        filename 47
        font 46
        format 43–44
            functional 43
            reverse chronological 43
            combination 44
        gaps 42–43
        honesty 41
        including quotes 45
        languages 45

layout 46
length 45
maternity leave 44
professionally written 40
rewriting if you don't have transferable skills 50
rewriting when changing occupation 48–50
what to exclude 39
words to delete 41–42
write in the third person 40
reverse chronological resume template 244

S
salary discussion with recruiters 117–118
salary field in online applications 78
salary negotiation 165–168
asking about salary before applying or being interviewed 167
not applying for jobs with low salaries 168
second interviews 139
skills 19–22
examples 19–21
employability skills 21
hard 19
soft 19

social media 225
STAR framework 70–71
STAR response tips 72
student resume 38
supported employment 186
Supported Wage System 184–185

T
T-Bar cover letter 63–68
templates 248, 249
training to improve employment outcome 213–217
effect of completing a certificate III or IV 213–214
effect of completing a master's degree 214–215
lower skilled occupations 215
micro-credentials 215–216

U
underqualified job seeker 173–174
unisex names 14

V
volunteering 235–236
volunteer roles 33–34

W
work history summary for your referees 247
workplace modifications 184

www.ingramcontent.com/pod-product-compliance
Lightning Source LLC
Chambersburg PA
CBHW050306010526
44107CB00055B/2124